To my son, and daughter,
my heart and my soul.

Acknowledgement

Many thanks to my best lifelong friend Nan Coulter for the great drawing at the beginning of each story. She drew the picture of me many years ago as a young girl. And to my great niece, Maggie. Using a page from her great-great grandmother's notebook, she hand wrote the title on the cover of the book. And to all those that helped create my wonderful memories.

A Memoir by Barb Colby

It was obvious from the first day of kindergarten that Laurie Ann was going to be a damn pain in the ass and it was going to be this way all through school until the day I would finally reach eighteen and escape my tortured association with her. I immediately disliked her little face drawn tight by hair pulled back into an aggressively perfect ponytail. Her tiny breakable little body was outfitted in this stupid little dress with a pokey starched can-can slip that made her look like an umbrella or a damn cake decoration. She was a major pain in the ass.

It only got worse once I started to see her in action. After the morning milk break our teacher, Miss Lockow, stood in front of the clustered group of confused newbies and demanded to know who didn't finish off all of their damn milk from those damn little milk cartons. I knew who, Laurie Ann knew who, everyone under the age of six knew it, but not Miss Lockow. And she was going to make sure that nobody had any damn fun until the guilty party confessed. But not a damn word out of little Miss Pain in the Ass. "Oh, for crying out loud Laurie Ann!", I screamed in repressed silence, "Just say you didn't finish the damn milk so we can get on with whatever we were supposed to get on with." But she didn't and I knew what had to be done. In the first of many obstinate moments to come, I stated strongly with grit teeth, "It was me. I didn't finish the (damn) milk. Now can we un-herd please?" Miss Lockow, with arms folded over her chest, tapped her foot on the ground, looked at my ruddy stubby Norwegian presence and stated she was pretty sure I drank all my damn milk. It was going to be a long life.

Flash forward through a steady six years of Laurie Ann and her shiny black baby doll shoes with those damn white anklets with flowers sewn around the edges. We were in Mrs. Harms' history class and of course she was sitting right next to me with the same damn pony tail and her perfect pencils that never had any damn teeth marks on them. Grrrrr.

It was November 22, 1963. Over the intercom at South Junior High School, we heard the principal call all the teachers to the front office and we were left on our own to commit social outrages on each other. When Mrs. Harms returned, she was crying. She told us what happened in Dallas TX and that President Kennedy was dead. We were thirteen; we didn't know what the hell to do. Then Laurie Ann starts to quietly whimper and puts her head down on her desk. I was stunned! Could this be a part of Little Miss Pain in the Ass that I hadn't seen before? Did she grasp the magnitude of what had just happened? Was she emotionally far deeper than I had ever given her credit for? I was dumbstruck. Laurie Ann slowly turned her tear streaked face towards me, reached out her hand to me and asked "Does this mean the communists are going to take my dog Fluffy?"

Damn.

Linda was eight years old when we were neighborhood friends for a very short instant in my life, but she taught me something that I'll always be grateful for and sad about. She and her mom and younger twin brothers and baby sister lived in the crummiest house on the block. The moms in the neighborhood would talk about the family while they drank coffee in our kitchen. That's how I learned that they were poor and that her dad was in prison, and they were on welfare. I got some of my best information about the neighborhood while sitting under the kitchen table listening to them gossip and wondering why some women had hairy legs and others didn't.

Linda and I got along great together and sometimes we would help watch the twins for her mom. One of the boys was cross eyed and their noses were always running. They seemed perpetually unwashed and dressed in ragamuffin clothes. But they were sweet kids with a natural sort of happiness in spite of life. All I remembered about her mom was seeing her sitting at the kitchen table in her bathrobe, her hair tied up with a handkerchief, smoking a cigarette.

There were five kids in our family and our bedrooms were upstairs on the second floor that was shaped like a big teepee. We were each given a specific step on the stairway that was ours to put our stuff on until the next time we went up and could take everything with us. This included clothes fresh from the dryer, toys and homework and whatever else we had left laying around the house for Mom to pick up. Mom designated each of the first 5 steps as one of ours depending on birth order, mine being the 4th from the bottom.

I had a glass piggy bank that was really shaped like a pig with a slot for coins perched on its back. My grandfather had given me a fifty-cent piece. This was a valuable item since we were not too well off ourselves, and I had always worshipped my grandfather which made it even more important. The coin was too big to fit through the slot, so it sat balanced half in and out on the back of the pig.

The piggy bank with the fifty-cent piece in it was on my step waiting for me to take up to my bedroom when Linda came over to play. Later the coin was missing. I was sure she had taken it and promptly told her so and that we were no longer friends. Well, time is a funny thing, and it seems that she moved out of the neighborhood shortly after that. I never even said goodbye.

Then we heard that the house they moved to caught fire and she and her brothers and the baby were trapped upstairs. Their mom got out safely, but the kids were found dead with their heads buried in a basket of dirty clothes. They were trying not to die.

Linda, I'm so very sorry. I need to say that. I need you to hear it. I'll never again place anything over the value of a friendship. Please forgive me. I was young and dumb. You were my friend. And now I know that sometimes you don't get another chance to make things right.

I still have your picture from the newspaper clipping. You will always be eight years old.

 We were playing runaway orphans in Julie's backyard on one of those crisp fall days. I remember it was fall because the leaves crackled and crunched under my knees as we crawled behind a pile of old wood stacked against the garage. We needed to hide from the authorities. Once the coast was clear, we wiggled our way out to hop a train to the coast. We ran into a slight delay in our travels as I realized I'd taken a large chunk of the old wood with me embedded in the palm of my left hand.

Finding it no longer to our advantage to be runaway orphans, my friend Mary told me her mom was a great sliver-taker-outer. Knowing slivers were not my mom's specialty, I agreed to be led to her kitchen for minor surgery.

It was a big sliver, and I was warned by Mary's mom that this was going to hurt. She instructed Mary to get something to show me so that I would be distracted from the impending pain. Dutifully, Mary gathered a stack of magazines. On the first magazine cover there was a picture of a circus clown. The next few I don't remember. But she held up the last magazine for a long time. She had become engrossed in what was happening to my hand.

The picture on the cover of the last magazine was of a soldier – a young soldier with a dirty face wearing a helmet. He was fighting some war I didn't know about in a land I'd never heard of. As I studied his face, I saw in his eyes the feeling I had when I got on the bus to go to camp and wondered if I would ever see my family again. I wondered if he cried at night too. And I wondered if he would die.

I don't remember any of the pain in the palm of my hand as the sliver was dug out. But I will always remember the soldier's face. I have scar on the palm of my left hand. And all these many years later, as I rub my fingers across it, I am reminded of the scar that was also left on my heart from a war I would grow up with. A war that would take my friend. A war in a land called Vietnam.

When I was ten years old my mom was pregnant with my brother. We were at the lake for a week when she was about six months along and the August days were as heavy with the heat and humidity as she was with child.

In "those" days pregnant women were doomed to dark blue or black maternity clothes that were designed to hide as much of their condition as possible. In an attempt to escape the uncomfortable temperatures, she loaded my three sisters and me into the rowboat one afternoon and we rowed to a small inlet surrounded by cool shade trees for a hidden swim.

Fully dressed, she slowly and carefully lowered her swollen body over the side of the boat into the soothing water. The rest of us threw ourselves in with great abandon and a sense of getting away with something we weren't supposed to be doing.

I don't remember much about our swim in the water, although I'm sure it was delightful. What I do vividly remember was the pandemonium that broke out after one of my sisters screamed that something was biting her toe.

Well, it was everyone for themselves. The previous moments of bliss were replaced by screams of panic and flailing arms and legs in now turbulent, fearful waters. It was sort of a 1950's version of "Jaws". I think it was then that I realized my mother was not the saint I had envisioned. No helping hand was offered to any of us. Please understand I'm not faulting her, for if I were, I would need to explain how I managed to use one of my sisters as a stepstool to get into the boat.

Once we were safely back in the boat with all of our arms and legs still attached, we drip-dried in the sun and rowed back to the cabin as if nothing had happened.

 In the summer my friends and I would go to Woolworths and buy ice cream drumsticks. Eating them was really quite a production. My particular method included eating the nuts off the top one by one, then peeling back the chocolate to expose the cold ice cream and a universal finish of biting off the end of the cone and sucking the ice cream out before devouring the sugar cone.

One Saturday I was last in line of friends to pay. When it came my turn I opened up my hot little fist and held out my entire financial savings. The clerk dispassionately informed me that I was a nickel short. Being too young to know how to handle this difficult a predicament I could only stand and stare, for what seemed an eternity, at the cone in my left hand and the two nickels in my right.

Then out of the corner of my left eye I saw a grey wool coat and an old thin hand as delicate and sturdy as the lace on the back of Grandma's couch reach over to me and place a nickel on the counter. "This is for the child's ice cream", the voice belonging to the coat said. I was ashamed and embarrassed and only hope I said thank you as I dropped my nickels and ran into the sunlight after my friends.

How I wish I could see her and thank her for that small kindness. If someone were to give me a million dollars, it would not mean as much to me as that nickel on the counter of Woolworth's in 1962. Maybe when I die, she will be one of the people who greet me on the other side. I won't know her face, but I will know it is her by her hand.

 One summer my parents took us to a friend's cabin on Maple Lake to spend a week with them. The cabin was red and sat at the top of a hill that gently sloped down to the beach. I was five so it felt like a far away magical fairy tale land instead of the small snake shaped mud bottom lake 30 miles east of town that it was. The four of us kids were all under the age of eight, so we spent most of our time sitting on the beach or slashing around in the water. It was our first experience with the great unexplored world of western Minnesota.

In the side of the yard there was a water pump with a long sturdy handle that was as red as the house. I hung from it like a jungle gym trying to get the water to come out of the spout. Dad picked me up and laid me over the handle like a dish cloth but it didn't budge. The grownups laughed and I was quite happy to be the focus of such fun even though it hurt my stomach.

At night the grownups would play cards and we would lie in bed and listen to them. I didn't understand their card talk but I loved the rhythm of the sound as they laughed heartily at what each other said as the cards shuffled and slapped on the table and the cigarette smoke drifted into the bedrooms.

One sunny afternoon we sat in the grass viewing all that was ours as we snacked on Hershey chocolate bars and drank six-ounce bottles of Coca-Cola. As the sun bathed our bodies and snacks, I remember how my Hershey bar melted down my fingers and landed on my knees and feet as I sat cross legged in the sand. This didn't stop me; I just picked up the melted clumps and ate them anyway. But I couldn't understand why the piece of chocolate between my toes wouldn't come off as I tugged on it.

Rather puzzled, I turned and raised my foot to my mother for assistance. "A blood sucker!" she screamed and quickly rolled off the beach towel that protected her from the insect life in the grass to avoid dealing with my slimy predicament. "Give it to your father!" Being new to blood suckers I didn't know enough to panic. I turned to my dad who calmly pulled it off my foot with a snap and a sting, folded it up in the Hershey bar wrapper and told me to throw it in the garbage.

As I walked behind the cabin to the garbage can I realized two things. First of all, things weren't always what they seem to be, and secondly maybe it would be a good idea to swim with my socks on.

I struggled into my teenage years the summer of 1962 at the lake during our family vacation. I spent most of the week desperately trying to hang around with my older sister and a group of older kids while they desperately tried to ditch me. At 11 years old I wasn't a really strong swimmer and my mother's rule was that when the water was neck high I was to go no further. My sister and her buddies were three years older and taller than I was and they used this to their advantage. I would repeatedly run into the lake with them with grand expectations of water fights and shrieks of delight as the boys would try to dunk us. But I was always stopped neck high as they continued into forbidden territory with their extra inches.

I never got the hint. I would stand stretched to the max on my tip toes and try to entice them back. "Hey guys! You should see this really cool rock I'm standing on." "Hey Guys! I think I see a leach." "Hey guys! Your mom's calling you." My memory does a freeze frame right there. I don't ever remember them coming back in. I don't know how long I stood and watched from afar. I just remember standing there, pruney, with blue lips watching a world that was not mine to have.

I still feel that way today. When I see women half my age that know how to wear makeup and can walk in high heels, I wonder how they learned to go so far out into the lake. When I see people who have become doctors and lawyers and nuclear physicists, I feel like I am eleven once again and standing precariously on a rock in the water up to my neck. When I apply for a new job, I'm sure they are whispering a plan on how to ditch me. Whenever I stand in a large crowd of people and my 5'1" frame is buried in backs and chests I just want to give up and head for shore. And whenever I have to ask someone for help at the grocery store to get something down from the top shelf I try to never start the request with "Hey guys!"

 When I was seventeen a foreign exchange student came to our high school. His name was Sam and we were instant friends. But it was 1968 and Sam was black. We were in a small town and I learned that year that it was filled with some small people. It was then that I knew I would someday leave that town.

Sam and I tried to pay no attention to the stares and with innocence I would never know again, we found in each other something better. To leave the town behind we would walk through a park that follows a river that defies conformity and flows north instead of south. To protect them from spring flooding the town's people built a tall earthen dike between the town and the river. We would walk the dike for hours and lose ourselves in conversation.

It was an important year for both of us. I'll never know what he learned from me, but I'll never forget what I learned from him. I had never been east of Wisconsin and Sam spoke of his time in Oxford England. The only accent I knew was Norwegian. But Sam spoke like a song with a rhythm and sweetness that rang strong with gayety and an openness that felt warm and safe. He spoke of his village in Uganda and his place among his people. I watched him dance under his first snowfall. We shared Sloppy Joes with pickles and the music of the Beatles and he taught me to swear in Swahili. He told me that one day he had many questions he would someday ask God.

I asked him to the Sadie Hawkins dance without a clue of the negative reaction it would bring. We dressed as a doctor and nurse. The contrast between his dark skin and white scrubs was wonderful and in the pictures that were taken at the dance he almost disappeared into the dark background with only his white scrubs standing out. I worked on the class yearbook, so I was able to keep the original photo taken by the school photographer. But the picture never made it to the yearbook. And when it came time for the spring prom Sam told me that he had wanted to ask me to be his date. But that couldn't happen because another date had been arranged for him. She was also an African foreign exchange student from another North Dakota city that was to be bused in as his date. Great planning had gone into effect to make sure he was not seen dancing in public with a white student again.

The year passed quickly and then he returned home. But the government of his country of Uganda had turned ugly and young independent thinking people like Sam were dying. And in a split second of time I would learn that I would never see Sam again. I hope God had the answers Sam so needed and deserved. Mine remained.

 The thing I hated most about being a little kid is that people were always sticking you places without telling you what to do. Every day was a new game but no one ever told you the rules. Worse yet, if you screwed up they had a right to punish you. It about drove me nuts. I remember several events of my youth that I wandered through in a haze hoping to survive.

The first day of Sunday school my mom dressed me and my sister up in uncomfortable clothes white gloves and all. She placed a nickel in each hand, drove us to a gothic type castle and dropped us off in a room full of strangers. After the strangers said stuff to us for awhile they had us pass this basket hand over hand down the row to each other. After that my older sister said it was time to leave. As she reached for my hand she found the stupid nickel still clenched in my hot sweaty little glove. She informed me I was going straight to hell for stealing from the church. Good! I thought, maybe there they'll tell me what I'm supposed to do.

And why can't adults sit you down and tell you not wrap your tongue around metal objects in the dead of winter? Or that it isn't a good idea to touch dog poop just to feel what it's like. Or that cold bacon grease looks like ice cream but is so not. Why must you experience that first hand?   Would it be so hard for them to tell you in advance about these things? I wouldn't think so. As soon as a kid can read a complete sentence they should hand you a manual.

I was five or six when Mom and I walked past a downtown store window with a wedding dress in it. "When are you going to get married Mom?" I blurted out. "Hush!" she reprimanded me and dragged me to the car. Well, nobody told me Mom and Dad were married. How was I supposed to know? I hadn't even been taught the "first comes love, then comes marriage, then comes me in a baby carriage" verse, which might have given me a clue. No, I was supposed to figure all this stuff out for myself.

And when the time came for my friend Candy and me to buy our first bras we didn't have a clue how to do this. We went to the third floor of Griffith's Department store, avoided the blue haired clerk, grabbed a bra off the shelf, paid for it (I think) and ran home to try it on. Well of course it didn't fit, way too pointy on the ends. So we decided to take scissors and cut out the pointy ends. When my friend put the bra on under her white T Shirt...well try to visualize it because I'm not going to explain any further. But the point is that it didn't have to be that way. I bet if there was a manual it would have had at least one paragraph on how to by a brassiere (my Aunt Vadrene call bras that and I thought it was such a funny word).

And it wasn't just me. In the sixth grade I was hall monitor the second day of school. I found a kindergarten kid standing at the exit door crying. I tried to walk him back to his kindergarten room. He looked up at me with panic on his tear streaked face and shrieked at me, "I already came here lasterday. Nobody said I had to come back again!" That's right kid; they think it's funny not to tell you the rules.

 At some early point in my life I heard my mother refer to one of our church members as a "drunken Presbyterian". So if I was ever asked what denomination I was, I would readily volunteer that I was a drunken Presbyterian. I don't remember anyone ever correcting me.

I never really got the big picture about this religious stuff. I had too many questions and no answers. In Sunday school we would learn about David being thrown to the lions. "For crying out loud!" I would scream to myself as the story was read. "Tell them whatever they want to hear, just get out of there." But the ending was always the same and it gave me nightmares.

Our local newspaper was called the Grand Forks Herald. At Christmas time in Sunday school we would sing "Hark the Herald Angels Sing". So were these newspaper employees just very gifted singers or honest to God angels? I needed answers.

"Now I lay me down to sleep. I pray the lord my soul to keep. If I should die before I wake..." Wait a minute! What do you mean IF? For crying out loud, there is no if! Someone please tell me I'm not going to die between 8:30 pm and 7:30 am, if it's a school night that is. Otherwise there is a longer stretch of danger in the night possibilities on the weekends. And there was really scary stuff.

Like "yea, though I walk through the valley of the shadow of death I shall fear no evil". I don't think so! If anyone told me they wouldn't be scared spit less in that valley, I wasn't going to buy it. And there just had to be an alternative route around that horrible valley! Somebody get a map!

Wonder how many existentialists started out as drunken Presbyterians?

When I was 13 years old Jim told me I looked great in a dress that did a pretty good job of showing off my developing reproductive assets. We were immediate friends.

The two of us shared Mr. Sinclair's 9:00 math class. Never did God produce a more stiff, formal, (does he even have a heartbeat?) kind of man than Mr. Sinclair. Despite this, one morning as we waited for Mr. Sinclair to make his entry Jim got up, faced the class and instructed us to burst forth in song the minute Mr. Sinclair came into the room. We were to sing "You are My Sunshine" using the harmonizing skills we learned in music class. I can still only sing the alto version of that song. In comes Mr. Sinclair in his suit and tie and we broke into song. When we were done with both versus the room was silent until Mr. Sinclair looked down at his math book and quietly stated that our song was greatly appreciated, his father had died the night before and would we please refer to yesterday's assignment. Jim just wasn't quite like the rest of us.

That summer he dove off a pontoon boat at Maple Lake and broke his neck. I bought him a get well card writing that I would see him soon. Before I could mail it to the hospital, he died. And so, as I would learn often happens in life, so did a piece of me.

During the early 1970's the world was changing. So was Grand Forks North Dakota. At least a little. Up until that point the YMCA was for men and YWCA was for women. Grand Forks tore down the YMCA, a shame to say the least, because it was a great old building. The YWCA became an annex to Central High School because of its proximity to the school. The city then renamed it the Y Family Center. For the first time this gave the men and women of the city permission to comingle with each other recreationally. One of the amenities of the new center was a small café offering nourishment to the patrons. In an attempt to pay for my college education, I worked the kitchen on weekends. We offered a wide variety of cuisine ranging from burgers to goulash with white buttered bread, pancakes and bacon to lemon meringue pie that 3 days later turned into whipped lemon pudding with fresh whipped cream plopped on top.

But I digress and will return now to the social evolution of Grand Forks. In order to partake in this fancy new community center, you had to buy a membership. One step forward, two steps back. All the rich kids were members. Their happy parents dropped them off Saturday morning to wreak havoc on the staff. My mother once told me that I was a bigot, a bigot against rich people. This job certainly didn't help my affliction. As I served up the daily special, washed dishes and ground up yesterday's food for its reappearance the next day, these little monsters destroyed the dining area. Favorite activities included loosening the salt and pepper shaker tops so the next unsuspecting diner would wreck their goulash. They would fill a paper cup half full of pop, stuff the other half full of napkins and quickly turn it over on the table so that when I cleaned up the table, well you get the idea. I was particularly fond of the ice cream cone stuck to the wall.

As proof of their enlightenment, the Y Family Center gave out a limited number of free memberships to poor kids. I have no idea how they were picked, but only the strong survived. Everyone knew who these kids were and they might as well have put a scarlet P for POOR KID on their backs. One of these "poor kids" was a brave young man who came up to the counter and established a summer ritual between the two of us. Burgers were a quarter at that time and it was plainly written on the menu board. "Can I get a burger without the bun for 15 cents?" he asked. Since I was majoring in social work he had asked the right person. In a millisecond I responded,

"Absolutely. I don't like the bun either and many people prefer to order the beef alone". "Then I'll have that", he declared. I pressed for details. "With the burger there are extras thrown in for no extra cost. Would you be interested in melted cheese, chips, pickles, lettuce, tomato, ketchup and mustard? We also include a large glass of ice water." He decided that would be acceptable. So, for the summer my "poor kid" came in every Saturday with his head held high and had a 15 cent "cheeseburger with no bun please". He always left me a penny tip. I loved that kid. And now if I am with someone who orders a cheeseburger, in the back of my mind I hear him whisper, "Without the bun please".

 Every Monday morning of my third grade year at Lewis & Clark Elementary we had Show and Tell. Miss Anderson would let one lucky kid a week get up and tell something wonderful that had happened in their life. I'd waited all year for something worthy of sharing with the class and it finally happened. My parents bought a new refrigerator. And it was a humdinger. It had special little cups in the door to hold eggs and a spot just for the butter. I could hardly contain myself. Miss Anderson was now going to gush over me, my news, my life. I would be the center of her attention, the center of her world. My moment had arrived.

Monday morning I rose to the occasion and proudly announced to the class, "We got a new fridge!" Unfortunately Miss Anderson was gazing out the classroom window lost in her own daydream and didn't hear a word I said. There was total silence, no response. The class of twenty five eight year olds looked like a still-life painting. I stood there for what seemed like a full school year and finally sat down in utter rejection. Miss Anderson eventually came to and uttered some lame remark to make up for her lack of attention.

What the Hell! I'm not sure what life enhancing, character-building lesson I took from that experience. Maybe I learned that a new fridge with a special place for butter takes a back seat to a grown-up daydream every time. Or maybe I learned that I better not count on the Miss Andersons of the world to validate my special moments in life. Maybe that life is just one big fat existential "so what".

All I do know for sure is that in 1959 we got a new fridge. And it was a humdinger!

 There are times I hadn't been a nice child. My neighborhood friend Mary fell into the ditch of cold spring water with her new doll and doll buggy and I laughed. I stole a pink girdle from my aunt's drawer once. It was so pretty. I skipped my piano lesson, kept the dollar and told my mom I'd gone. Once I cheated on a test and felt so guilty that I wrote "I will not cheat on a test ever again" one hundred times. I hadn't even been caught. Sometimes I faked being sick so my mom would spend extra time with me. We had her divided five ways, so you had to take special measures to insure attention.

Sometimes I did fun, naughty things. Once when my dad was sleeping on the couch and snoring like a bear in a cave, I painted his toenails red. Fortunately, he found it equally hilarious. In the sixth grade I put a rubber fake pile of throw up on my teacher's desk. At the lake, when we were fifteen miles from nowhere, I hid my mom's cigarettes. She didn't see the humor in that one.

All in all my sins were fairly minor. Except for the time...well never mind.

You know how some kids are always bringing home stray cats and dogs. Well, I always brought home dead birds. I would carefully lay them out in a Kleenex filled shoe box and memorize how they looked. Then I would leave them for a day and check back to see if they had moved. Most of the time I was sure they had, which meant something mystical or heavenly had happened.

I was always looking for a miracle. I would lie in the grass looking up at the clouds for hours, knowing that Jesus would show himself to me if I was thinking pure thoughts. I would try to heal cuts and scrapes by the laying on my hands, just like a lady in a movie I watched. My sisters thought I was a little strange and maybe so. But I don't think there is any harm in keeping your eyes open. It would be a shame to miss the miracle when it happens.

When I was 12 years old I overheard my parents talking in a hushed conversation about my cousin, Doug. Doug was about 16 at the time and in trouble again. He was caught selling prophylactics at the school. Hum, I thought to myself, I must remember how to say that word so I can find out what it means. Prophylactics – prophylactics. This was a strange word to memorize and would take some effort. Prophylactics – prophylactics – prophylactics. Once I was sure I had the word down, I needed to come up with a way to find out what it meant.

I hated being left out of the loop on these hushed issues, but that's the way it was. I was on my own and I knew it. So I decided I would casually bring it up in a conversation. Maybe someone would say something that would give me clues to figure out the meaning of this word.

I practiced in front of the mirror in my bedroom "So" I said leaning slightly to the left, "I hear the department store is having a sale on prophylactics." Or, maybe a sports angle would work. Resting my elbow casually on the dresser I tried out my new idea, "Guess I'll go watch the softball game". I hear they're handing out free prophylactics".

I could think of nothing else. If Doug was selling them, then they must be something we're not supposed to have. Maybe beer, which could be it, prophylactic beer. Or they could be a brand of cigarettes. That could be it too. Prophylactic smokes. I was getting desperate.

Maybe I should try the direct approach and ask. This was a scary plan but my options were few. I'd just go straight to Mom and ask her what the heck a prophylactic was. But I feared she might slowly turn into a pillar of salt right before my very eyes. I saw a woman do that in a movie once and it wasn't pretty. Asking Dad was just a dumb idea. At the very least he would tell me to go ask Mom. At the worst…well since I didn't know what the stupid word meant I didn't know what the worst could be. So just forget it. Prophylactics – prophylactics – prophylactics.

Later as an adult who now was in the parent's role, I was asked by my young daughter that very question after watching a 1980s "safe sex" ad on TV. I wasn't about to repeat the past and leave my child out of the loop. So, I carefully explained what it was. "Oh!" she exclaimed, with such understanding on her young face. "I heard about those on the school bus. You mean a rubber!"

 Our town of Grand Forks ND sat along the Red River. Often the river would flood in the spring. I had things backwards and thought that the neighborhoods were sinking into the river instead of the river climbing the gradual slopes to the houses.

It was this river that taught me terror. Even when it was behaving itself it was a symbol of death to me. My mother would warn us not to go near the river at any time. I'm sure she issued the normal "mom" kind of warnings, but I heard worse. I was convinced that if I got within twenty feet of the water I would be sucked in against my will and dragged into the bottom where I would drown in an eternal whirlpool filled with other stupid kids who defied their parent's rules.

My grandparents took us out one spring afternoon for a ride to look at the flood areas. As we drove down the dirt road that ran through the park that was now half underwater, I dug my nails into my grandfather's shoulders and pleaded to go home. He assured me that he would not drive the car into the water. I thought to myself that he must be unaware of the power of the river to reach up and pull us in, Buick and all. How powerless I felt in the backseat. How grateful I felt to reach our home which was far enough away from the river to be safe. How surprised I was at my grandfather's belief that he was more powerful than the Red River. It wasn't until the flood of 1997 that I found out how real my fears were.

Mimi's grandparent's farm was a major part of my childhood education. I would spend weekends with them whenever I could. I loved it there. It was my chance to be Timmy and pretend Lassie was there by my side through my explorations and discoveries.

One of my favorite attractions on the farm was her uncle, Sonny. He was a big hulking Scandinavian who delighted in making us giggle. He would come in from the field after a long day covered by sweat and earth and a wide white grin that would explode like a sunrise through the black dirt on his face. The chase was on. We would squeal with delight as he attempted to catch us and smear us with the day's work covering his overalls. We would scramble into the tightest corner of the kitchen that was as big as a school gym and secretly hope he would be able to reach us.

One evening Mimi and I decided to view the farm from the top of a large haystack. We felt like mountain climbers as we challenged the prickly face of the cliff. Once on top we marveled at the view. This must be how God feels. As we watched the sun begin to disappear and feel the air begin to cool our sun warmed skin, we realized that the ground had become very far away. How in the world had we gotten up here in the first place?

We started to scream our brains out in hopes of notifying superman or anyone else in the ear shot of our dilemma. Then out strides Sonny and the thought of his strong arms lifting me down from our dilemma was worth the humiliation of all the other grownups as they laughed at our predicament. His hands were warm and strong and sure. And if he had asked that nine year old girl to marry him, without even asking her mom, she would have said yes.

It was Halloween. I'm not sure how old I was but it was around the time I was eye to eye with some adult belly buttons. Mom had a baby at home and had hired some poor teenage girl with nothing else to do but make a little money taking me and my younger sisters around the neighborhood. In anticipation of the sugar filled night I had been practicing my new Halloween speech in front of the upstairs bedroom mirror. Having no say in my custom choice I was dressed in some awful princess outfit with a parka over it. Halloween was tricky up north and cold that year. But I was just as glad to hide the frills under it.

We set out right after dinner to Mrs. Barnes house two doors down. She answered our knock with a bowl of wonderful junk we weren't always allowed to eat and ready to tell us how scary or cute we were. This was my moment. My eyes glued to her bowl of candy I loudly proclaimed, "Trick or treat, money or eats, but if you don't give me some candy, I'll kick you in the seat." Pretty proud theatrical debut for me! Well, I did not receive a standing ovation. She gasped at my request with wide eyes, choked on her gum, and then spit it out into her hand. Yuk!

Honestly, I'm not sure if I realized I made a boo-boo or if I was just pleased with the way things were going. Needless to say, the underpaid babysitter was not pleased. She grabbed me by the hood of my parka and dragged me down the steps. My confused sisters (a bunny and a clown) had no idea what had just happened. With a cracked nail polished finger in my face, I was sharply informed that I was not to open my stupid mouth again for the rest of the short excursion around the neighborhood. I'm pretty sure that's when I began developing my sense of humor that occasionally steps beyond the line of a good idea.

 There's nothing like the Cold War to give a kid early paranoia. Once a month at Lewis & Clark Elementary School they would shuffle us down to the bowels of the school and have us huddled in rows on the floor with our knees pulled in tight and our heads down to save us from destruction. The nuclear threat was very real to us. So was the fact that if you were unlucky enough to wear a dress that day, dying was less of a concern than the fact that in that un-lady like position your underpants were showing.

As we sat there on the cold floor I spent most of my time thinking about my mom and my baby brother at home only three blocks away. If that horrible man who would beat his shoe on the table ever did decide to kill us all, I had a plan. I knew I could outrun most of the teachers watching us in the hall. As soon as I saw a break I would head for the nearest exit and beeline it home. I had heard that after the button was pushed you had 20 minutes before it hit. I had to see my mom before I died. That was all I knew. I would rather die with her then be saved in the basement of the school. What a sad way to grow up.

Mr. Baaken hadn't meant to confuse or fluster me. All he was doing was teaching 6th grade health class and I wasn't even in his room. But when my friend, Becky, tried to explain what she had learned it got all messed up. "The reason we come out the way we do has to do with our genes uniting." she explained. Well, that's not what I heard. To someone who had grown up wearing mostly this particular pair of pant, jeans had only one meaning and the thought of the jeans uniting was almost enough to blow a fuse in my underdeveloped mind. I frantically tried not to envision the front zippers of these jeans in a close-up personal position. I sensed that the general geographical areas were right but had a dickens of a time trying to understand how the Levi Company had control of how we turned out as people.

In this day and age it would be enough to inspire me to bring a civil suit against my elementary school gym teacher, Mr. Wilson. But times were different then and our lessons in life were, more often than not, learned in painful silence and stored for future distress or growth. Maybe I should thank him. He is probably partially responsible for my strong feminist stand in life.

I digress. Back to the story. In 1961 girls were not given the opportunity to play in many sports. Running was one of the exceptions which later proved to be of great help as the boys reached puberty. But after years of playing baseball, the boys were seasoned veterans of the game. Mr. Wilson got his jollies every spring by staging a game of softball pitting the boys against the girls. It was quite clear by that point, and to all that knew me that I had the DNA of a tomboy pulsing through my study Norwegian body. As a result all the girls in their little pink dresses with can-can slips looked to me with great hopes to bail them out of this nightmare and win the game single-handedly. And I felt it was not only my personal responsibility to do so, but my chance to right all the wrongs done to all the girls and woman of the world. It was quite a big job for a 12 year old girl.

 One Christmas when I visited Santa Claus at Woolworths, he was old and white and wrinkly. The next year he was bigger and had dark brown eyebrows and a full young face. Well I had heard the theory about elves helping Santa out and all, but I was starting to have some serious doubts. There was other evidence to support my skepticism. For instance, why were my presents from Santa addressed to me in my mom's handwriting? It was true that the bowl of cheerios we left out on Christmas Eve was always empty in the morning, but why were there never any footprints in the snow or reindeer poop in the yard?

After much thought I approached my mom one quiet evening when we were alone. It was high time she knew the truth. It wasn't easy to watch the disappointment on her face as I explained all the reasons why there couldn't really be a Santa Claus. She valiantly attempted to convince me that I was wrong. I could see in her face the need to hold on to her illusion of old Saint Nicholas.

I had been wrong to tell her. Who was I to burst her bubble? So, in the end I smiled and patted her lovingly on the cheek and reassured her that indeed there was a Santa Claus. I would wait a few years before we discussed the Easter Bunny.

I had my tonsils removed when I was five. I brought my clown doll to the hospital with me. As they prepared me for the surgery the doctor asked me if I would like to take my doll into the operating room with me. I gladly accepted the offer of company on my journey into the unknown. When I woke up in recovery the clown lay beside me with gauze wrapped around his neck. I wish I could thank the doctor for that small act of kindness.

The nurse on the other hand was a different story. As I lay on the table, this cold, immense woman dressed in white approached me with a kitchen strainer and placed it over my nose without my permission. She told me she wanted me to smell the perfume Santa had given her for Christmas. As the smell of ether floated into my nose sleepiness drifted thru my body and the world slowly became unreal. I could hear her tell me that I was going to have a wonderful dream. This was not truth in advertising. My wonderful dream consisted of being tied down to a wooden board with pumpkins circling my head. These weren't ordinary pumpkins; they had maniacal faces and were reciting my name over and over as if in a trance. To make matters worse, lightning bolts were flashing up and down my sides so I couldn't move an inch.

I remember finding the courage to squeak out a "help me". The nurse, now millions of miles away, replied, "you don't need any help".

The first thing I asked my mom when I awoke was, "how many tonsils do you have in your body?" I was relieved to know they were all gone now and more relieved when she reassured me that they could not grow back. Good thing I got lots of terrific cards and presents from everybody.

Scott was a big kid. A really big kid. The biggest kid in the school. And Scott loved Laurie Ann, the littlest girl that could possibly exist. He loved her a lot. So, one day in Mr. Martin's 4th grade class he wrote her a love note and attempted to pass it to her. Mr. Martin saw what was happening and grabbed it from one of the kids in the chain of delivery. And then he started to read it to the class. Scott let out what I would later learn was called a primal scream. He threw his head back, his eyes disappeared into his reddening face, his mouth opened and out came the scream. "THAT IS MY NOTE, GIVE ME MY NOTE". But Mr. Martin continued to read and so Scott continued to scream. The class froze.

Then Mr. Martin dropped the note and came at Scott's desk with a thunder. Mr. Martin was an average sized guy in a suit and tie. But at that moment he didn't seem to register the size difference or how it would affect his next move. He grabbed Scott by the arm and yelled at him that he was taking him to the dreaded principal's office. Scott had a different plan. He wasn't leaving the desk until he had the note. Mr. Martin pulled at Scott and Scott wrapped his hands around the top of the desk showing that he had no intentions of going anywhere. Mr. Martin no longer looked like Mr. Martin. He no longer looked like our teacher in the suit and tie. He had morphed into what some of us knew to be an angry father and none of us were happy about that! The tussle began. Scott's desk was making noises like the monster that ate New York. The kids in the desks surrounding Scott's were now swept up into the wake of the disaster. They were panicking and scrambling to flee the desks that were balancing on 2 legs, as they screeched across the classroom floor.

Then Mr. Martin started to drag Scott backwards, still in the desk, still screaming. At some point Scott and desk were separated. Defying all logical rules of physical possibilities Mr. Martin picked Scott up from behind and started for the door. Scott raised both legs and arms and did a spider plant on the door frame. Dear God would this never end! Mr. Martin pushed and turned and somehow took the understandably emotionally distraught kid to the damn principal's office. In the classroom sat 28 bug eyed, messed up 10 year olds. It was either something we had never seen before or something we had seen in our own homes. Either way it took a toll on those of us left in the classroom that confusing and horrible day. Scott had to return to that classroom alone. Scott had to come back to face the other kids. To this day I am saddened and angered by the memory and regret that I didn't know what to do, what to say to Scott to ease his pain. I hope someone did. But it wasn't me.

It wasn't that I was afraid of going to bed – I was afraid of dying! And that is precisely what would have happened to me if the "thing" under my bed got a hold of my ankle. So, I would start at the doorway to my bedroom and run full speed to a safe distance from my bed and leap onto it. Then I would position myself dead center in the bed so that if the "thing" decided to reach up, my arms wouldn't be hanging over the edge.

I was afraid of a lot of things when I was young. Like what would you do if puberty hit and you only got one boob, or what if your mom died or something and didn't tell anyone how to wash the clothes, or what would happen if all the things in your head started coming out of your mouth and you couldn't stop them?

The basement was a particularly horrifying place to visit. We had an extra bathroom way in the back, down a dark hall past the furnace. The toilet seat cover had a picture on it of a man flushing himself down the toilet. Above his head it said "goodbye cruel world". This poor man haunted me. I tried never to go in that room and see his tortured face.

Could a person really fit down there? What if you got stuck halfway?

But the scariest thing ever was when my friend Kathy told me her versions of how babies were made. I wonder if the Greyhound bus company ever got any other calls asking for the fare to "never-never land".

It was Mr. Larson's 10th grade Algebra class to be exact. I was a fairly good student with mostly A's and some B's in school. But not so much math. And certainly not the ridiculous branch of Algebra. Through some sick cosmic joke I ended up in Mr. Larson's higher level math class. It didn't take him long to figure out my mental math defect and proceed to publicly torture me in front of the entire class on a regular basis. Example: He would pass out the exam results and announce the highest score and who earned it (Jim G.) of course. And then he would simply state "and we know who got the lowest score".

Another time he informed the class that on that day we would be playing math games. He said that I might want to sit the games out and he had thought about letting me keep score but it might prove to be more than I could handle. So, one day as he stood next to me, in front of the class, repeatedly tapping the chalk on the blackboard and insisting I find the answer to a stupid problem, I let loose on him. I glared at him and then informed him that Algebra was completely useless to my future plans and a total waste of my time here on earth. I also made sure that he was clear on the fact that not only did I not understand it, I didn't want to understand it and I was not going to use up any of my life's energy trying to learn it.

He told me he liked my spunk and gave me a D.

My father was a handsome, wild young man who came from the "wrong side of the tracks". I have a great picture of him wearing a white t-shirt with a pack of cigarettes rolled in the sleeve. He was a boxer to boot with a killer jab and a smile to match.

My mother was a delicate, proper kind of girl who was the daughter of a local lawyer. In the picture I have of her, she is shyly leaning against a tree in her cardigan sweater and bob hair cut looking like a debutante.

Now whenever I am having difficulty explaining my behavior or a strange approach to life, I simply acknowledge the fact that I can expect nothing else. It would be opposed to the laws of nature if I weren't occasionally off the wall. What can you expect from someone that has the combined genetic makeup of Rocky Graziano and June Allison.

Don't ask me why but in grade school we referred to our first kiss as being "branded". Dave branded me one cold night at the Elk's Park skating rink in a snowbank. There was no soft mood music or panning away to the treetops. As I recall, his lips were cold and wet and his nose was running. Not a good intro to passion, but it was something to talk about at the next slumber party.

I remember my first long kiss. I was around thirteen and all I could think about was how I was going to breathe, and wondered if you were supposed to move your head around like they did in the movies. And do you move all the time or just once in a while.

Closing your eyes was another issue. Who does something for the first time with their eyes closed! And if you decide to close your eyes do you do it before you make contact or after? These were not the kind of questions you asked your mom. But once I did ask her if you had to be married to have a baby. The answer was yes.

 In 1966 I got my first real pet. I don't count birds and fish. I bought my dog for $1.50 from a kid one block away. She was a ball of white fur with a black eye and my mom said I could keep her if I named her Terryton. That year there was a cigarette ad that showed a person with a black eye saying "We Terryton smokers would rather fight than switch". So Terryton it was, but we called her Terry. She was my best non-human friend. Mom told me that when I went over to a friend for the night Terry would sleep by the front door waiting for me to come home. For six years I had the good fortune of her company.

Two houses down lived tiny, old Eva Berg. I didn't know that each night she would leave leftovers in a small bowl she would hand craft from aluminum foil on her front porch for my dog. Terry would eat both with great enthusiasm. Eventually this killed her. Despite my tears and the empty spot next to me I couldn't find it in my heart to be angry with kindly Eva Berg. She loved Terry almost as much as I did.

The minister of the Presbyterian Church called my uncle on day and told him he needed a favor and would he come to the church at 3:00. My uncle showed up with five other puzzled church members to find themselves as pall bearers in a funeral for a homeless man who came to town hiding in a box car on the Great Northern freight train and died with no one to identify or mourn him. Reverend Shew conducted his funeral service with the six pall bearers to witness this man's coming and going. Humanity is at its greatest in the small delicate corners of the heart.

Christmas 1968. The year of our Chevy Chase Christmas. The day before Christmas our family of nine, three generations of extended members, embarked on the worst holiday of our collective lives. One by one we succumbed to the worst case of stomach flu any of us had ever or will ever again suffer. Those of us that were pre symptoms attempted to set up a triage of care for those that were semi alert and stretched out on beds and couches and chairs illuminated by an uncared for tree of lights and unwrapped presents. The victims found themselves desperately waiting for the bathroom door to mercifully open for entry of the next emaciated pajama clad sad sack with emergency bowl in hand. At one point before Mom and I had fallen victim to the scourge we attempted to seek help from the emergency room. It was a blind, desperate attempt to save the family. As my stomach started to remind me that I was not superwoman and was about to join the half dead, the admitting person asked, "Was this an accident?". Those who know me will not be surprised with my snarky answer. With a look in my eyes both desperate and homicidal I retorted "Oh surely not!

We've planned this for months. Deck the halls with bowls of vomit fa-la-la-la-la."

In the sixth grade Sherwin asked me to meet him at the Dakota Theater and we would see a movie together. It was my first date. I made the mistake of telling my mother. She thought it was very cute and told my grandparents, aunts and uncles, neighbors and everyone within a ten block area that was willing to listen.

Of course, Sherwin stood me up. But that was of little concern to me since I had invited all of my friends to show up just in case I needed them. My dilemma was how to save face when I got home. So, I told my mother that everyone in Sherwin's family died and he was the only one left to make the funeral arrangements so he couldn't make it to movie. I think she bought it.

My grandmother is 96 years old. Her life consists of a single room in a nursing home. She thinks she's living in her home on 32nd street and it's 1943. She looks at her wall and sees dozens of pictures of people she has shared this world with for so many decades, but she doesn't remember who they are. I go to see her and she is smaller each time. She was once such a strong and powerful woman. Now her tiny body is trying to surrender as her spirit tries to escape her worldly prison. One of the pictures on the wall is from Christmas 1952. We are all there. You can almost smell the turkey and dressing on the table, hear the wrapping paper crumple on the floor. I am two years old and grandma is in the corner of the picture holding me high as if to present me to the world. One of her handsome sons is smiling. She doesn't know on that Christmas day he will leave this world soon after. But on that day we are all smiling. I would learn as I grew that Grandma's life was always hard, both by life's hand and her own inability to seek out the good and hold on to it. I would learn that she made life hard for all those around her. But in 1952 we were all smiling. And Grandma knows who I am. So, I like that picture best.

On Highway 81 just after the A&W drive-in and just before the cemetery was "Lowell's Body Shop". Since no one had ever explained to me what a body shop was, I figured it was where they took you just before they buried you in the cemetery.

I would always try to be reverent as we passed by in the car and try not to think about what Lowell did to the bodies in there.

I was one of those "good" kids mothers hope they will get after all five pregnancies. But no one is perfect. Mom took particular care of her fingernails. They were long and curved and always brightly painted with shiny red nail polish. She kept the nail polish in the medicine cabinet above the bathroom sink. Having nothing to do one day, I took it down to simply admire the bottle. And then to simply admire the brush filled with the wondrous grown-up stuff, and then to simply admire the pretty design it made as it dripped from the brush down to the white porcelain sink, and then to simply admire how smoothly the brush glided along the surface of the sink, and then to simply admire how wonderful the sink looked completely red, and then to simply believe that my mother would find my latest creation as marvelous as I did.

Without giving it any intellectual thought, I always figured that Grandma's hair just grew naturally with perfect soft cottony white rows of sculpted waves and covered with a hair net with tiny pastel beads in it. It always looked the same. But when she landed in the hospital with pneumonia I learned differently.

My perception of what was normal was hardly based in reality. For instance, I was pretty sure I was the only person in the world that had a butt. We were a modest bunch in my family and I was sure that even if someone else had one, mine was the only one that had two sides to it. We were only allowed to refer to this particular part of our anatomy as a "seat", which always made me wonder about the expression "please take a seat".

When I was a girl scout we made one of those things you put your bills or notes on. It had a square wood base with a very large nail sticking out of it on which to impale your papers. For some reason it was on the couch one day and I sat down on it with the intense vigor that kids have at that age. Needless to say I stuck myself good.

I ran into the bathroom to survey the damage, which wasn't easy considering the location of the wound and the fact that we only had one small mirror over the bathroom sink. Balancing on the edge of the tub I managed to see what I'd done and get off the tub before my eyes filled up with those black spots you get when you think you are going to throw up or faint. Since I was the only one in the world with a butt I naturally couldn't tell anyone. I sat funny for a while and quietly healed. I never told anyone about that – until now.

 We live in a town with an airbase. It is 1968 and I am in the 10th grade and it is time to file into the auditorium for an assembly. The speaker is a military man. Important, I think. He talks to us and we are all expected to listen, or at the very least, pretend to listen. I stop hearing his exact words and I find my mind is interpreting his intentions instead.

I hear him saying, "You will all do what we tell you to do. You will know that we speak the truth and you will be glad when we send you to a country you are only beginning to know about and you will die. You will believe that we are right and they are wrong. You will not ask questions".

I see the faculty rise and start to applaud because they agree or because they are spineless. Then the kids start to follow the leader and clap out of habit or boredom or the knowledge that after the clapping is done they can leave. But they clap none the less and make this over inflated costumed man look more important and dangerous. I stand because I have to. I stand because I don't know yet how not to. But I don't clap. My hands are clenched and shaking and my arms are stiff by my side, my stomach is sick. Inside my head I am screaming, "What's wrong with you people? Don't believe this fool!" It takes forever for the clapping to end or is it only that the seconds seem endless? As I try to leave I am dizzy with the conflict raging inside me. I know like I have never known anything before that I am right. But what if I'm not and they are and I am the fool?

 When my friend and I were 18 we started traveling around the country in whatever beat up car we had available and whenever we could save up enough money to do so. It was 1969 and we headed to Mexico. Not the real Mexico but Tijuana. We were young and dumb and full of fun and bought a lot of stuff. We bought bongo drums, and a little bottle of tequila with a worm in the bottom whose spirit would never be released into the hot humid air. We bought a doll with fruit on its head and a wooden box to hold hidden treasures. And then we bought a sombrero the size of a small UFO. At the end of the day we crossed back over the border on foot looking a bit like mules on the way to market. When we arrived back at our car the spending spree turned into a logistic nightmare. On our odyssey across the country we were using our car to sleep in to save money. So our UFO sombrero that was the size of a passenger didn't quite comfortably fit into our limited living space. So we sold everything we bought at half price to people passing by us on their way into Mexico so we could get into the car with a little wiggle room. But we kept the bongo drums.

We also drove through Montana. We were 5 feet tall, hair in braids, wearing bell bottoms, moccasins and smock tops. One afternoon we found ourselves in a small town in the middle of a million miles of open road and easily that much open sky. We entered a local general store and lollygagged around looking at all the odds and ends in the store. It didn't take long to realize that the few locals in the store were staring at us. We attempted to smile and say hi but only received suspicious looks and no responses. Quickly becoming uncomfortable we grabbed something to drink and headed toward the counter to pay when we noticed the local sheriff was posted at the front door. For the first time in my life I was afraid of someone in his position. With his arms crossed over his chest he made no comment. We hurriedly left the store and got into our car. He followed us out and closely tailed us in his squad car until we were miles out of town. You see, it was during the time of the Manson murders. We looked like the young girls that had committed those horrible crimes. So in their fearful eyes we were potential murderers. Simply by the way we dressed.

 I never really thought about it but I figure I always loved both my grandmas. They were very different from each other. One read books and was a gentle, proper sort of woman. The other one drove around in a black beat up Buick with lawn mowers and ladders sticking out of the trunk and mattresses and stuff tied to the top. She had rental property and considering some of her renters it wasn't too surprising that she had become a "tough old broad" as I once heard her referred to. She was short and stocky and walked as is she was trying to push through a wall. There was no denying that a hard life had made her hard herself.

Sometimes on Sunday afternoons she would come by our house and pick up whoever was out in the front yard doing nothing and take us to the Dairy Queen or around town as she ran her errands. On one of these excursions, when I was about six or so we stopped at a greasy spoon place called "Phil & Lil's". I don't remember what we were doing there, but as we left I heard the gal behind the counter say, "There goes a mighty strange one". I wanted to beat her up. How dare she call my grandma names! It didn't matter that she was fairly accurate in her description. This was my grandma she was insulting. I felt hurt and angry and embarrassed. And there was nothing I could do about it. I wondered if Grandma heard her and if Grandma was embarrassed or angry.   I wondered if I was as mean as that waitress because even if I didn't say it, I sometimes thought it too.

Years later I heard someone say, "It is okay if I insult my family but you are asking for blood if you insult them". That helped a little.

 I was about 8 years old at the time. I was in Grandma and Grandpa's 1958 Buick (AKA the Black Beast). Long before I turned 8 there was no doubt to anyone that I had 100% of the genetic makings of a Tom Boy. I was standing in the back seat as we drove down University Ave. I'd thrown my arms over the bench seat between the two so I could pretend to drive.

I started singing a new song I'd learned. It goes like this.

Reuben, Reuben, I've been thinking.
What a strange world this would be
If all the men were all transported
Far beyond the northern sea!
Reuben, Reuben, I've been thinking.
Life would be so easy then!
What a great world this would be,
If there were no tiresome men!

Relax guys, I was eight.

Anyway, after my rendition I posed a question. "Women have the babies and take care of the babies. Why do we have to have men. We could just do away with them." That got their attention. They stifled their giggles as they turned their heads to the center to look at me. It took them a minute to decide what to say and who was going to say it. It was Grandpa. He calmly responded by informing me that you need the men to make the babies. This made no sense to me at all. The men did bring home money for food and stuff so that must be why they had to be around. They watched me in anticipation as I pondered my next move. After a pregnant pause (pun intended) my jaw set and eyes focused on thought I replied more to myself than them, "I bet there's a way around this."

I spent a good deal of my formative years wishing I had been born a boy. I dressed like a boy, tried to think like a boy and attempted to adopt a nickname that would prove I was a boy. But puberty wasn't convinced and I started to grow boobs anyway.

I'm getting ahead of myself. While still in hooded sweatshirts to conceal my long reddish-blond hair, I frequently asserted my defiance by beating up any willing neighborhood boy. Teddy was usually more than willing to oblige my aggressiveness and on a fairly regular basis we would find ourselves in someone's front yard performing a well perfected wrestling hold on each other.

We would usually draw a fair crowd of observers as the kids passed on their way home from school. After we had spent ourselves we would part friends and head our separate ways in a condition of disarray. My appearance as I rounded the corner to my house was one of tangled hair interwoven with leaves and grass, my pedal pushers twisted sideways with the knees grass stained and sometimes torn. I remember one day in particular when one of my plaid tennis shoes completely disappeared.

For most of my early development I thought it was disgust and loathing that my innards felt when thinking of boys. I eventually change my approach to life, with the help of puberty and Jeff. He was beautiful and wild and wore his hair like the Beatles and I was in love.

I remember the day as if it were yesterday, okay maybe a little longer ago than that. I was at my first seventh-grade sock hop. Lacking in a wardrobe for sock hops, I sneaked out of the house in my older sister's yellow wool skirt and matching mohair sweater with pearls stitched to the front. I surprised myself with how nice I looked and secretly liked the new image. The gym was lined with high expectations, of what, we knew not, but somewhere in the deep recesses of hormonal growth our bodies were starting to whisper in our ears.

The details of the party are lost to history except for one dance. The only person in this world that could stir my newly emerging hormonal emotions sauntered up with unbelievable coolness and asked me to dance. With my heart pounding, my palms clammy and my mouth shut tight for fears of saying something really stupid or having bad breath, I danced my first slow dance with the only true love of my life. "Blue Velvet" was playing as I entered into womanhood, there in the arms of a 13 year old dream.

Our family moved into our home in Grand Forks in 1963. Over 55 years can turn the plaster, paint, windows and doors of a house into a second skin, the bones, muscles and heart of a family's collective memories. It's a decision of the brain, made out of necessity, not of the heart. It's a logical decision requiring all of us to deal with the emotional sadness of separation in our own way. Gone now are Mom and Dad. We have gently and lovingly bundled them up into our memories and carefully stored them in our hearts. It's time to say goodbye whether we are ready or not. How odd it is to think that some other family can just move in and claim our home as their own. A house is much like a chameleon in that respect. Without changing a piece of its structure, it becomes a vessel for an entirely different collection of memories for a new family. So, we will say goodbye to each emptied room filled with the spirits of our past and close the front door with the familiar squeak and the final creak of the front porch. But we know that regardless of who moves in, it will always be our home. We will graciously allow the owners to move their furniture and belongings into the house, but it will be on loan from us. We will drive by and from the outside looking in we will hope that they are enjoying life and loving our home as much as we did.

It started out as an adventure, a Nancy Drew book with me as Nancy. The car that backed out of the school parking lot next to my 1956 Ford Farlane left a very distinctive dark yellow streak on the side of my car that was recently purchased for $210.00 from a wealthy couple who won a new one. Few people in Grand Forks were brazen enough to have a paint job like that so I knew I had a chance of tracking down the perpetrator. I did a stake out each day before and after school watching for the vehicular criminal to return to the scene of the crime. And one day, there it was. It was obviously someone who thought he and his car were something special. I didn't really know one car from another, but I could tell that this car had been pampered and cared for. Was my car somehow less important? I think not. Pleased with my sleuthing skills I copied down the license plate number, called the cops and learned the name of the offending driver. The scratch on the car would cost $50.00 to repair and I would get satisfaction. I presented my completed task to my father and never expected what was to follow. Dad got up from the couch and said "Let's go!"

Oh no, what have I done? My great Nancy Drew experience was transformed into a stomach churning event. Dad drove me downtown and parked on the street in front of a two-story building destined to be included in the upcoming urban removal plan. There was a paint store on the ground floor and dreary apartments above. Dad instructed me to go up and get the cash while he waited in the car. I walked up the dark staircase that smelled of many years and many lives. The moment I stepped into the apartment I was consumed by the knowledge that I could do nothing to alter the outcome of this. I could have turned and left, been wise beyond my years and ended it right there, but I knew Dad would accept nothing less than me to return with the $50.00. And I wasn't that brave, yet. I was paralyzed by the moment and played it out as if I was an actor on a stage, programmed to play the role of the villain. And I did. The owner of the car was just a kid my age. He was every bit as proud of his car as I was of mine.

No, even more so.

I could tell by the apartment that the car was probably one of the few possessions that validated who he was. His mother was a defeated looking woman sitting at the kitchen table with her large black purse in front of her. There was a red bandana handkerchief tied around one of the handles. That stupid $50.00 was a huge amount of money to these people and all it was to me was a victory over a perceived villain. The three of us made no eye contact. It was painfully silent. We shared separate moments of embarrassment and shame.

I've tried to tell myself that this experience molded me into a more compassionate, insightful person. And maybe it did. But it doesn't ease the cringe of that night.

My grandfather told me that money itself is not good or evil; the value of money is defined by what you do with it. I was ashamed of what I had done with it. To say that what happened that night was not my intention is not a valid excuse. My mistake was to not think first. I was so caught up in my adventure that I had forgotten to look forward to where the trip would take me. Breathe, think, decide, then act. I would try to never forget the human heart again. To do so is to cause pain both to others and myself. Lesson hard learned.

 I killed Nat King Cole. Nobody could tell me differently. Early in my religious education I had decided that it was my moral obligation to pray for everyone in trouble and every bad event that was happening in the world. I heard the news that Nat had lung cancer and I forgot to pray for him and naturally he died.

It was fairly obvious that God needed guidance. There were wars, starvations, disease and my recent discovery of secrets behind the doors of some of the neighborhood houses. It was up to me to set God straight. This was a big job for a 10 year old but since it was obvious that no one else was taking on the task I had to step up to the plate. It wasn't that I thought I was powerful, quite the opposite. I had discovered the concept of guilt and it was frighteningly uncomfortable. I became consumed with the need to do everything I could to cover all the bases and it was exhausting.

And I had questions. If this concept of prayers getting answered was real, how many prayers were needed to save a particular person or event? Was it different for each case? Maybe someone had only five people who gave a darn about them and they needed seven. Or was only one person needed to plead for divine intervention? I needed answers!

This was very time consuming. How did you fit in homework? How could you justify going to the neighborhood swimming pool with your friends when the time could be better spent saving someone's life with a swing vote? I started praying every time I heard sirens and asking God to bless every old person I passed on the street. I would have driven myself crazy if I wasn't acutely aware of the fact that going nuts would have interfered with my praying time. So in the end I found a loophole. Each night before bed I prayed, "God bless everybody in the whole wide world. Amen".

 My first serious grown up kiss happened in the furnace room of my parent's basement. I couldn't swear to it but I'm almost positive Mel Carter's "Hold Me, Thrill Me, Kiss Me" was playing on the record player in the other room. And for the twenty seconds of bliss I'm almost positive he was singing the words "They've never stood in the dark with you love...when you take me in your arms and drive me slowly out of my mind". This kind of insanity I could get used to!

In those few short...long...seconds I was transformed. Not only did I no longer harbor any desire to be a boy, I was now acutely aware that my body possessed the same chemical power of the rockets that sent John Glenn out of this world. In those remarkable twenty seconds I no longer listened to the midnight train whistle, I was on that train racing towards a new life in some far away romantic place like Paris or Minneapolis. In those twenty seconds I became worldly and insightful and, well, horny. I was sure that when my family saw me emerge from that encounter they would scarcely recognize the new me. Of course no one noticed. But many years later I can still occasionally be found in the furnace room in my parent's basement, remembering.

 By any 16-year-old's standard Andy was the most gorgeous senior at Central High School. And it didn't hurt that he was from a wealthy family and drove a blue Mustang. Every weekend of the summer about 200 or so teenagers would descend upon one city block that was home to the local Drive Inn called The Kegs. True to its name, The Kegs had two huge wooden kegs at each the corners of the building. And I do mean huge, they were over a story high and an actual working part of the building. We would circle around the block like the cast in an old western for hours on Friday and Saturday night in hopes of something happening, anything happening! One circle of cars would travel clockwise around the block and the other counter clockwise. We would drive with our windows down and spend the night in a slow stop and go social intercourse with whoever was adjacent to us at the time. In Grand Forks North Dakota in 1968 this was Nirvana.

Now if the social gods were with you, your car would be in exactly the right spot as someone was pulling out so you could get the coveted prize of an actual parking spot. You could then order from an extensive cuisine of sloppy joes with or without cheese and pickles. With an actual parking spot and food to boot, you were among the blessed for the evening. At that point in time I was driving a 1956 Ford Fairlane. It was yellow and white and round, bringing to mind a lemon of mixed origins. It was purchased for $210.00 from a couple who won a new car in a drawing. One degree of separation from winning a new one was fine with me. I loved that car.

One fateful night I was driving with my friends Becky and Janice who were in the back seat drinking beer out of a pop can, when who should suddenly appear in front of me? You guessed it, Andy. Well, I was all a twitter. As my mind raced with ideas of how I could use this momentous occasion to my advantage and somehow connect with my future, he abruptly stopped his mustang in front of me and I rear-ended him. Perfect! Really, I mean it. This was perfect. As he stepped out of the car in beautiful slow motion I saw my future with him unfolding before my eyes. I knew that the moment he saw me he would know I was the woman he was meant to spend the rest of his days with. How we would laugh as we would tell our grandchildren how we met that fateful night at the Kegs. How we would cherish our memories of sharing sloppy joes with pickles and cheese. I stepped out of the car to approach my destiny. I will never forget the first words that Andy said to me.

"You   stupid   idiot!"   Oh   well,   never   mind.

 My freshman year at the university I defied every rule I could remember including the one about never hitchhiking or you will end up dead in a ditch. I barely had enough time to leave the beginning stages of perfecting the skill of ignoring good advice when my aunt Vadrene saw me hitchhiking and promptly reported my behavior to my parents. Uncharacteristically my dad got involved in my life and with a compassion that I was unprepared for asked that I please never do that again and surprisingly offered me cab money any time I needed to get anywhere. He said that all I had to do was ask, which of course I was both incapable of and unwilling to do.

One summer afternoon I accepted a ride from the devil himself. It would prove to be a two mile ride that would last a lifetime in my memory of lessons that I could no longer afford to ignore. This abhorrent form of life started to tell me about what can happen to young women that hitchhike. He was not trying to warn me of the dangers. No, he was enjoying the stories. You don't need the details; let your imagination fill in the blanks. "Do you hitchhike often?" the creep inquired. The appropriate answer would have been, "apparently one time too often". But I was frantically repeating "oh God oh God oh God" in my head. I was learning that women sometimes have an early warning system that automatically starts flashing a "warning Will Robinson" sign in front of their panic stricken faces. Unfortunately, it often commences after you are already in far too deep.

My grandmother was a dark woman who specialized in the under belly of life and seemed to thrill at telling her grandchildren horror stories of what humans were capable of doing to other humans. She would save newspaper articles about these unfortunate victims and give them to us to read. God forbid I should have a grandmother who secretly sneaked us sweets. One such article relayed the story of, what else, foolish young girls hitchhiking and ending up brutalized and dead in a ditch. But what really got Grandma going was the part about how the killer cut off their fingers and kept them in his pocket. Okay, so you know what was running through my mind as we completed mile one of the ride.

As I looked ahead down University Avenue I was well aware that at the end of the campus the road headed straight for the flat, unpopulated fields of North Dakota. It appeared I was going to end up in a newspaper article my grandmother could cut out and keep in her little scrapbook of horrors. I started to wonder if I would survive a jump out of the car doing 35 miles an hour. I gripped the handle of the door and realized that there was one stop light between me and the loss of my fingers. As the sick son of a bitch continued with more stories I silently screamed "red light – red light – please God let there be a red light". If God was busy that day and the light was green I would take my chances with the pavement racing beside me and try to remember my judo teacher instructions to roll. "Red light, red light, please God let there be a red light." God was apparently in town that day and let me keep my fingers, 'cause the light turned red and I jumped from the stopped car from hell and ran for my life. I never asked my parents for cab money. I never hitchhiked again. My grandmother remained a crazy old lady.

 When Grandma was sick she said, "Go to the library and get books for me to read". Knowing her appetite for mysteries I asked, "How will I know what you've read"? "That's the easy part", she whispered, "I've turned back the corner of page 13 in each of the books I've read".

Many years later, I took my mother to the library. She had never known the secret. So like kids on a scavenger hunt we set out on a quest to see if Grandma's books were still there.

In the company of Agatha Christie we sat on the floor surrounded by stories and softly touched the corner of the pages and told Grandma we remembered.

 I was nine or ten at the time. Young enough to leave my parents for a weekend but without realizing what homesickness was. Young enough to still hope that maybe, just maybe if I was lucky I could still turn out to be a boy. My friend Janice told me one day that her parents agreed that she could ask a friend to go to Detroit Lakes for the weekend with them and she picked me 'cause her best friend Becky couldn't go. Janice's parents were old parents and reminded me of the picture of the lady and man with the pitchfork standing in front of their house. Harold wasn't exactly a barrel of laughs and Mable was short and square. She always wore a dress and never got mad at us even when we tried to make taffy in her kitchen managing only to make a huge mess which we left for her to clean up. Her older brother was quite a bit older and made me nervous. I don't know why. But he wasn't going with us and that made me glad. He could stay in that dark garage with the stuff bobcat he killed and was so proud of. It made me want to cry to see the poor cat forever frozen in one place. She was so pretty and sad and creepy all at the same time. I wanted to grab her, bolt from the garage and set her free. But she couldn't walk anymore so there she sat.

So off we went in their family station wagon for an exciting weekend adventure in Detroit Lakes. Riding in a car was more fun back then because we got the back of the station wagon and could pretend it was a fort. Nobody wore seat belts. If you lost a kid in an accident, oh well, one less to feed is the way I think it was. I had never been to Detroit Lakes before. It was what I now know to be a pretty typical Minnesota lake resort town. We got a motel right on the main street which leads down to the lake where there were rides and food and a pavilion where the teenagers went and drank and did crazy stuff, or so I was told by Janice.

We unpacked and tried to feel like those crazy teenagers with our very own motel room. The world awaited. I didn't realize something was wrong until we went to the Deer Park where you could feed and pet real deer. I had never done that before so I was pretty excited and pleased with life right then. But as I stood at the entrance looking at them looking at me I knew things weren't quite as rosy as I thought. "What?" I thought. "Help me out here, I'm a kid and haven't figured anything out yet". Mabel gave me this look. I didn't have a clue what it meant but it was sweet and warm and made me feel like I'd brought Grandma with me. Then Harold whispered something in her ear. He didn't look as sweet and warm. They nodded at each other and paid for my ticket. Then I got it. I didn't have one stinking penny on me. What the hell. Boy did I feel stupid. Money! Nobody thought to give me money!

And now I was the poor kid that they had to take care of and pay for whenever we did anything. And I mean everything all blasted weekend long. Food, tickets to the stupid Deer Park, rides at the park by the water, treats – "no thank you I'm not hungry". I was! But far more powerful was that I was ashamed. That wasn't a new feeling for me. But I didn't like the fact that I was getting used to it and now I had to feel it every minute of this long never ending weekend. I didn't know what to say to Janice. I didn't know what to say to Harold and Mabel. I just wanted to go home. I didn't want to stay at the motel and pretend to be a teenager, I didn't want to have to order from the right side of the menu checking for the cheapest item and I didn't want to be there. I just wanted to go home. But I couldn't. I would like to say that this was some life enriching moment for me. That it made me a more self sufficient adult who always brought cash or never left home without a credit card. But it wasn't. It was just awful. And I knew that Janice would tell Becky and everyone on the whole stupid planet that I didn't have any money and probably that I was no fun at all and acted weird the whole time. Well guilty as charged. I plead no contest. You win world. Janice didn't ask me to go on a weekend trip with her ever again. She took Becky.   And that was o.k. with me. Really, it was.

 When we were growing up we would go on summer vacations, just like most everyone else. Except we went with Dad. He looked at most of life as a challenge. With all 7 of us stuffed into the car filled with cigarette smoke and wind slapping at our faces through the open windows we would head off to wherever. Dad found his fun trying to see how long he could drive on an empty tank of gas. He was pretty good at it I must admit and he took great pride in proving all of our anxieties wrong. But we would plead with him anyway to stop sooner with cries of needing to go potty, or complaints that one of us was torturing the other in the back seat. But that didn't persuade him, no not Dad.

One time stuck with me all through these years later. Things were looking pretty grim for us as we finally really ran totally out of gas. Mom was chewing on her lip and tying her handkerchief into nautical knots while we little ones were bemoaning our fate of having to walk to our inevitable demise. Just as the car gave its last sputter we coasted a few more feet and found ourselves at the crest of a hill that suddenly became a slow roller coaster decent. We gently rolled down to the bottom where, low and behold, a gas station awaited us. He turned and grinned at mom and said "Never fear when Dad is here".

It had never occurred to me before but it did certainly straighten me out when I saw the look of shock on a friends face when I casually told her the story. Before she could utter the words, I realized that when I was eleven years old I was molested by a doctor. It's funny how our subconscious protects us in a mental bubble wrap. Not so funny when the bubbles pop. At that moment of clarity I had a tsunami of emotions imagining how I would have felt if this had happened to my daughter and wondering how my mother may have felt. But it will take more time for me to decide how I felt and feel about it. Some events become engraved on a person like the words chiseled on a head stone.

This is how it happened or at least how I remember it happening. I was eleven years old in 1962 and in order to go to summer camp you had to have a basic physical. The common check list of childhood diseases, check your eyes, ears, nose, a "popsicle stick" to check out your throat and any questions or concerns from Mom. In those days you actually dressed up to go to the doctor. Mom wore a dark colored straight skirt, blouse and jacket with heals and a purse. She looked good but definitely not the same Mom I knew at home in capri pants and a sweater with a crushed up handkerchief tucked in her sleeve. I remember what I wore that day. I looked quite fetching in a light blue checked number with the navy blue plastic belt. Even as a tomboy I occasionally enjoyed pretending I was a girly girl.

My memory starts with the doctor's exam room. Mom is sitting next to the exam table with her legs crossed and hands folded in her lap twisting her handkerchief. I'm laying on the table with no clothes on, maybe a drape over me, I don't remember. I hear him ask if I had started menstruating yet. She replies "no". He gets up and closes the blinds on the window that faces the street. The room darkens. There are no colors just shades of grey. He sits me up and puts the stethoscope on my chest and asks me to take several deep breaths. I do, but the breaths are jagged and come in halted steps, up and down, up and down. I'm shaking. Then he has me lay back down and puts my feet in the stirrups. He turns on a bright light at the end of the table and I can feel the heat on my skin. Then he touches me with his fingers. Only on the outside but not what I now know to be the professional touch of a doctor doing what a doctor does. It's slow and gentle. Then we go home. Nothing is said. It's the early 1960's and you just don't talk about things.

Years later I remember my mom referring to that day and saying "I felt so bad for you, you were so nervous". That moment stuck with her too but I'm not sure for what reasons and now that she's gone I'll never know. And I probably will never know just exactly how I feel or what to do with those feelings even if I did.

I was a tomboy. In grade school I loved to fight. I mostly fought boys. I didn't know there was another option at that point. So I fought boys. Mom didn't like it, not one little bit. She'd give me the look, but it never worked. She knew she had no control over my pugilistic tendencies. So she'd fold her arms over her house dress and fear for my future. I loved it, except for once. Sarah's cousin was visiting. And she was a brute. She was like some New York street kid and I was no match for her. But she heard that I was the kid to beat, and she came at me like a John Deere tactor. And as I was getting the living Captain Crunch beat out of me under a bush Mom watched from the porch. You know how you scream when you are having a nightmare, but you aren't doing it out loud in real life. That's what I was doing. I was silently screaming for her to save my sorry ass from certain death. But she had resigned herself to this behavior and let me work it out. But after that I learned my lesson and knew enough to avoid the girls and stick with beating the snot out of boys.

Around the block from our house was Elks Park. In addition to the 1950s playground equipment that would today seem as dangerous as sending your child into a construction site, there was an outdoor swimming pool. My friends and I would spend most of our summers there in a pruney state of bliss.

The pool area was divided into three separate sections. There was the kiddie pool that consisted of two thirds part screaming kids and one third part waste products. Then there was the main pool that wasn't much different in makeup from the kiddie pool but because it was much bigger and there was more water in it the ick factor wasn't as noticeable. As would-be teenagers this is where we hung out most of the time. A regulation in some book required the that life guards stand up from their perches every two hours, blow their whistles signaling a mass exodus of the pool so that they could check for dead kids trampled at the bottom. Then when everyone was sure some little kid wasn't down there the second whistle sounded and we had permission to push each other back in said pool.

The third area of the pool was for diving. That's all you did there. Describing it as diving is a stretch, more panicked jumping in than actual diving but that's just a technicality. There were two short diving boards flanking the high diving board. And it was very high, especially when you were only three feet tall.

Now I probably went to the pool from the time I was eight to sixteen years of age. In that time period I started out in a one piece choo-choo train swimming suit. Trust me I paid for that one. Thankfully I eventually graduated into a pink, I'm too sexy for my own good, two piece suit that got the boys a'lookin. However, this story is about what happened at the diving pool during the choo-choo train era.

All the kids would line up to climb the high board for a chance to prove that they weren't scaredy cats when in fact that is exactly what most of us were. About six kids would be clinging the ladder nose to butt as we slowly ascended to the top of the summit for a chance to once again defy death. The ladder is where I took the most abuse for having a swimsuit with cartoon trains on it. There was no getting away from the fact that the kid behind me was looking at the caboose on my caboose. Coming from a family of five kids I had no choice but to tough it out with that stupid suit until I was gifted with my older sister's suit when she out grew hers. I could then pass on my misery to my younger sister with no thought about what she was about to endure.

Now back to the story. After jumping off the board we would promptly swim to the edge, climb out and start the agonizing process all over again. I had obviously not heard about the concept of free will at that point in my development. One day as I doggy paddled my way to the edge of the diving pool I saw a kid next to me in the water doing a very unique swimming stroke. It looked a bit like a slow dance or a butterfly. It was very graceful, and a bit odd. I got to the ladder at the edge of the pool, climbed out, got back in line nose to butt to again hope that it would be a girl that would be behind me this time, please. When I jumped back in, there was that same kid still doing his strange underwater ballet. However, this time was different. Before I made it to the edge of the pool the adult world woke up. Even under water I could hear the hollering and then the water turned into a churning cauldron of big bodies and children fleeing the area as if they were in trouble for sure. But they weren't. That little boy was. He was drowning and I watched. I watched twice. He didn't die. I'm really glad he didn't drown that day. The right thing to say is that I'm glad for his sake but if I'm really honest about it I'm glad for my sake. Because over the years it's hard enough to remember that day as it is. If he had died I don't know where I would be able to put that memory so that it didn't haunt me.

Nature verses nurture. If you are a parent of more than one child this debate is pointless. We know the answer. Our kids are a living combination of both forces sprinkled with the genes of some distance crazy ancestor thrown in to baffle the parents.

We had a son and a daughter born 18 months apart. My son John was a calm thinker, too smart for his own good. I soon became aware of his tendency to over analyze most of his day-to-day moments. My daughter, Jennie, on the other hand was a, free spirited kid that went quickly from moment to moment.

When they were of the age to be taught life lessons, we started learning how to safely cross the street. Tightly holding their tiny hands we would approach the corner. Each time I would repeat the same rules to ensure our survival and safe return home to catch Sesame Street before lunch. And I stress that every time I repeated the same rules to both. On one particular day we journeyed out to practice our skills.

At the next corner we went through the drill and I said that we could now cross the street. My son quickly pointed out that there was a car coming from several very long blocks away. He informed me that we must wait since we did not know the exact speed of the car or distance of each block to safely determine when it would arrive at the corner on the other side of the street. My daughter, with a look of free abandonment chimed in "I just close my eyes and run!"

Five minutes after her birth, I knew my daughter was going to be a handful. Sometime after her first word and before constructing full sentences, I knew that she had a quick temper and a strong willed, stubborn approach to life. Scary combination. Once she was old enough to understand, I made an attempt to teach her that she had options, I told her that when anything happened in life she always had two choices; you can choose to make things better or you can choose to make things worse. I knew better than to push the issue and that with time she would chew on the advice and hopefully use it. Not long after my words of wisdom Jennie was off on a tangent about something. She hollered and stomped and flailed around like an electrified butterfly and theatrically ended the event with a march into her bedroom followed by a loud slam of the door. Within seconds she threw open the door, stuck her head out into the hall and with a glare of defiance strongly stated, "I CHOOSE TO MAKE IT WORSE!"

Well, at least she made a choice.

She looked so small standing there on the corner on her first day of school holding her Care Bear backpack. Her cowlick arched her bangs over her eyebrow. She hadn't yet realized it was there, hadn't yet learned to hate it and try desperately to subdue it. Seeing her brave little excitement and holding her tiny little hand as we watched the bus approach was making me emotionally dizzy. We had practiced for this moment. Everything was going so well until the bus doors opened and I started towards the steps. She froze, looked at me and we both forgot all the talks we'd had about what this day would be like, about how much fun she'd have and the new friends she'd meet. I picked her up and carried her to the first empty seat. I did all the right Mom things, everything I knew I had to do, while inside I was fighting the panic that was welling up in me. "I don't want to go!" she cried, "Mommy don't make me go!" I tried to quickly reassure her that everything would be okay, that I would see her soon and that she was going to have fun. I could see in her eyes that she wasn't buying any of it any more than I was. She was breaking my heart. I had to unfold her fingers to free them from the knitting of my sweater.

As I left the bus I fought the urge to grab her and run from the bus screaming, "You can't have her! She's my baby and you can't get her, ever! Please let me keep her forever five years old." My mind flashed to all scary things that the world would throw at her, the sadness, the hurt, the disappointments, and the pain. I was suddenly all too aware of the fact that I couldn't save her from them. Life can almost be too much to bear at times. All I wanted to do was run home with her and make an amazing fort out of a box that thought its only function was to surround a new dryer on delivery day.

I left her on the bus and waved bravely as she disappeared down the road. I ran to the car and tried to stem the painful swelling of tears. Without putting thought before deed, I raced after the bus and followed it to the school. I pulled into the parking lot and watched the parade of little human beings leave the bus and start their lives away from their moms and the familiar surroundings of their homes that had been their whole world so far. I could hardly breathe as I waited to see her step off the bus, so afraid that I would not be able to stop myself from rushing to her to stop time from taking her away from me. But she got off the bus just fine thank you. And as she did, the little girl in front of her took her hand and they disappeared into the school together. Then I cried. A good, long, well deserved cry of release and relief. That day we both took first steps. Jennie's was a step off the bus. Mine was an understanding of this day as simply one of many steps I would watch her take in this lifetime of steps we would separately take together.

My son John had a repetitive pattern of ditching school. When he turned 14 I realized I was no longer in control and had developed a "wish me luck" attitude. John was a tall sturdily built kid with long black hair, brown eyes and olive skin. I, however, was a very short red head with green eyes and a complexion that screamed STAY OUT OF THE SUN.

During this time my husband was a letter carrier for the local post office.

I needed to go to the school for a meeting that would establish a plan to keep him from ditching. All I thought was, well good luck with that one. However, I needed to show them somehow that I was a responsible parent. I went into the office and addressed the school secretary behind the counter who was in charge of trying to figure out which absence slips were authentic, and which were forged for the day.

I simply stated who I was, and that I was there for a meeting and that I was John's mother. My appearance was a surprise to her and she laughed and blurted out, "That's hard to believe!" I reassured her that I was indeed his mother. She winked at me and said, "It must have been the mail man." With a sly hushed voice, I leaned in and whispered "It was". I then turned to leave her with a hilarious look of surprise on her jaw dropped face.

 I worked as a social worker in long term care facilities when my children were young. I was new at being a mom and learning as I went along. The men and woman I worked with were seasoned souls and taught me much about the path of life. One of them was Eleanor. She was 104 and had lived in our town long enough to remember playing with the native children along the beaches of Lake Minnetonka. She was at the end of her journey. We visited and she shared with me that she wasn't afraid of dying. She believed she had lived a good life and would go to heaven. Her only concern was leaving her children alone. Her children were in their 80's. I realized at that moment what motherhood really meant. A mother's love is an emotional shift in your very being. It is a permanent realignment of your existence. I think of her now and again and her simple statement of eternal love. A mother's love.

My two years of working the front desk at Deaconess Hospital taught me more about human nature than all the years of studying to become a social worker. I was 18 and still pretty unaware of life outside of my family and friends. I had much to learn.

My natural instinct was to assume everything was all right if you just didn't admit to it not being all right. That's not how it works in a hospital. Reality came rushing through the front door on a regular basis and I was not ready for it.

So I learned. I learned a lot. For instance, you need to know when not to say "Don't Cry". A very small child was in the Emergency Room with no parent. This kid had ample cause to be crying and if he had not been crying there would have been serious concerns for his health. I went to him and held his hand and then stupidly uttered "Don't cry". The nurse walked in and looked sideways at me and asked "Why shouldn't he cry? He's hurt!" Had I time to examine my motives I would have realized that my response to his pain was not out of concern for him but simply that I wanted him not to cry to make me feel better. Lesson learned; it's obviously ok to cry but more importantly to let someone else cry.

Irish McNally was the well know alcoholic in town. This was before treatment centers and an understanding of the devastation of the disease. Back then he was simply a drunk. He once passed out in a ditch on a frigid North Dakota night and ended up with several amputated toes from frost bite. I walked by the Emergency room one evening to see Irish strapped to a bed. He was in the thralls of withdrawal and hallucinating that snakes were falling from the ceiling on his trapped body. His screams were horrifying. I found myself cemented to the floor tiles, unable to walk away from the complete torture this poor man was experiencing. I felt hands on my shoulders that turned me away from this man's private hell and directed me down the hall to the elevator. The guiding nurse said nothing to me. That day I learned when to turn away, when to walk away or be lead away when you aren't on top of your game.

My assigned spot at the admitting desk faced the front door of the hospital which was the portal to all misery in the city. It also faced the only elevator in the hospital. The doors to the elevator would open up like theater curtains and you never knew what play was about to start and who the actors were going to be. I was 18 and really not ready for what I saw. A mother brought in a baby that wasn't breathing. An admitting clerk grabbed the baby and started mild breaths to keep the baby alive. The baby made it. I wasn't so sure I was going to however and just prayed I'd never be on either side of that drama. Lesson learned; keep your fingers crossed or better yet, take a CPR course.

There were times when the elevator brought down all the grieving families in one wave of anguish. It was natural to look up when the elevator doors opened. As a result there was often eye contact before I could turn away and try to hide from the huge pain I didn't want to see. I realize now that they were so consumed in whatever had just happened that even if I was dressed in a hippo costume they wouldn't have seen me. I quickly learned to just keep doing what I was doing because at that moment I had no role in what was playing out.

One day I admitted a guy whose name was Johnny Cash. I didn't mention the obvious for whatever reason. He looked at me and thanked me for not making a joke about it or breaking into song about Folsom Prison. To this day I try to never state the obvious about a person.

You never knew what the day would bring. A man approached the desk one day, looked into my naive 18 year old face and said "I need to see I doctor. I think I have the clap". Well, I wasn't exactly sure what he was talking about but for some reason I knew not to ask. This lesson was about being careful to never to ask a question that might elicit an answer you really didn't want to hear.

Part of my job was the intercom. I was to page doctors, make short announcements and the like. I was taught to use "my bedroom voice" so as not to make the patient's day any worse than it already was. Well up to that point in my life I hadn't had the opportunity to practice *that* voice in real life but I did figure out how to say "Dr White, paging Dr White" in a low soft (sexy?) voice. A guy I went to school with was in the hospital after having his appendix removed. I went up to visit him and after the first minutes of polite back and forth he said "Hey Barb do you think you could introduce me to the gal on the intercom?" Apparently, I was a quick learner!

We had something called the Death Book. When someone died you entered the date of death and the person's name in a large legal size book. It had been around for many years and reminded me of something you would find abandoned in the corner of an old library. It was a history book of sorts of the last days of the town's citizens. The first time I added a name it was of a 14 year old mentally challenged girl that I babysat for off and on. I remember staring down at her name written out carefully in my handwriting. It was the last time I was to feel connected to her. So I learned how not to cry when you really wanted to.

I mostly worked the 3-11 shift. A woman came in to be admitted to the emergency room late one weekend night. She was a waitress at a local bar. Her hair and clothes were disheveled. As I started to take her information she started to tell me her story. She needed to tell someone and there I was. That night she left the bar with a guy she knew. He drove her out into the country where they met another man in a car. Her "date" then sold her to the other man and left. She was raped and dropped off outside of town. She walked quite a distance to the hospital to get help. Her distress was obvious but in a quiet, numb disbelieving way. I finished my part of her long admission process and sent her up to the emergency room. I then walked to the back of the office where two women from the office were already talking about her. They let me know that if she didn't want to be raped she shouldn't be working in a bar. She had asked for it. It was that simple to them. It was not so simple for the waitress. I'd like to think times have changed. And they have, but not enough, not enough.

The farmland around Grand Forks was successful in great part because of the migrant workers that came up from the south to work the fields. Late one night a young migrant woman came in with a very sick baby. Mom was scared and the baby was far too quiet. I started to take her information and when it came to the insurance question she told me she didn't have any. Since this was a new occurrence in my training I went to the back office to ask a staff person how I was to handle this. I was told to send her away. She explained that the hospital would never get their money so it wasn't worth it to admit her baby. Then she finished my instructions off with her thoughts on the worth of migrant workers. I stood there in disbelief that not only was this her answer but knowing what I was now expected to do to this poor mother. After a momentary pause in the hallway to regain my composure, I executed my first act of rebellion against the system. Knowing I could lose my job and almost hoping I would I walked back to my desk and in a hushed voiced finished the admission process and sent her and her baby up to the emergency room. That day I learned the importance of standing up at the right time and doing the right thing.

The Northern Railway trains ran right through the middle of town. It also ran right through the left foot of a 14 year old boy that figured if he rolled under the train fast enough he could get to wherever he was going just a little faster. After his long recovery he came back to visit the staff that had become an important part of his trauma and fight back to his new normal. He was excited and upbeat and even proud of his new prosthetic shoe and wore it as his badge of courage. His enthusiasm and youthful hopefulness were infectious. After all he had been through he managed to leave everyone at the hospital smiling. I still think of him when life hits me upside the head.

I also answered the switchboard. It was the old fashioned one with many cords to connect and disconnect. Mostly the calls were from family members asking to talk to grandma in room 350. But in amongst all these benign calls were the ambulance calls. I was literally answering 911 calls with about 30 minutes of training. I was way too young to be taking those calls and I hated it. I was sure I was going to be responsible for killing someone and that was a reality. I received calls that would go something like this. "Help! My son shot himself in the chest! Send an ambulance!" Sir, can you please give me your name and address?" And this would be the answer. "Go down County Road

12 'til you see the barn that's falling down. Take a left and follow the dirt road 'til it comes to the tree that got hit by lightning and go over the bridge but watch for the tire tracks that veer off after the cabbage patch and then go to the first farm on the left." Try to write all that down as a father is frantically screaming in your ear to hurry up. Then I would hit the alert button and give the ambulance drivers the directions. Picture me praying "Oh please God don't let me screw this up! I'll do anything you ask just don't let this kid die because of me messing up." Well he didn't die but I almost did. I finally got to the point that just sitting down in front of the switchboard caused my entire body to start violently shaking. That was when I decided to go back to babysitting.

So what did I learn? Well, I wasn't sure what I was going to do with the rest of my life but chances were slim to none that I had a future as a 911 operator.

If I had to sum up all I learned during my first job at Deaconess Hospital it would be this. Life can and will be hard so you better get used to it. And we are mostly tough enough to get through it. And we had better be kind enough to help those that aren't.

 When I was 24 both of my maternal grandparents died in an accident. Words, being as inadequate as they can sometimes be, I will limit them to simply say that I was devastated. At their funeral we sat in a packed church with many towns' people showing their respect for two people that through their simple unadorned dignity brought our town to a better place simply for having been here. My grandparents affected me in ways that I am not an accomplished enough writer to explain. But this story is about my father.

We had a pretty normal relationship growing up. Emotions and the awareness of each other took a back seat to everyday life. But when the funeral ended and everyone left, I couldn't. I sat in the pew of the gothic chapel of the First Presbyterian Church and literally could not move. I had nothing left inside of me. It had all been swept away in one moment of one day and I didn't know how to get it back. I stared at the place where the two coffins had been and tried my best to change the events of the last week. I think I really believed that there was some way I could undo this tragedy, reverse the unrelenting movement of time and somehow get them back.

I would experience the same emotion the day the family women met at their house to systematically and painfully dismantle the physical day to day lives of my grandparents. As I walked into the door of their home and saw my aunt emptying out the dishes from the dining room hutch I fought the volcanic urge to scream, "Put it all back. Don't touch one more thing so that when they come back it will all be waiting for them." A home filled with all of the little items of our memories that in some small way explain who we are. The Hummel dolls, the photos, the dish Grandma always put the ribbon candy in at Christmas. There was Grandpa's chair and lamp where he sat and finally surrendered to my mother's pressure to watch "All in the Family" and reluctantly admitted that we were right and it was a great show. And Grandma's handkerchief tucked into the corner of the couch where she sat and knitted mittens each year before Christmas for the Salvation Army. Grandpa's Edward R Murrow "I Can Hear It Now" records that he would play for me to open my mind to the world outside of Grand Forks.

But that day in the church as I sat alone in the empty chapel after everyone else had moved on to the next step of separation in the mourning process we had to travel through together. I watched my father come out of a corner of the church and slowly walk towards me. He sat down next to me in the pew and didn't say a word. We just sat together. It was one of the simplest yet most powerful moments I had ever experienced with him. At some point he took by hand and said, "We'll walk out together." Never had words been so life saving. I needed his strength to move both physically and emotionally past a moment in life that had almost stopped my heart from beating. I found a part of my father that I didn't know was there. And that moment would carry our relationship to a place I didn't think was possible, one of love, compassion and respect. A relationship that I desperately needed to help fill a wound that I was sure would never heal.

 I was bright enough. I received good grades in everything, with the exception of biology. With little foresight I postponed the inevitable Biology 101 class until my senior year in college. I knew we were going to have to cut up poor creature that at one point was happily going about their business until they were caught and transported to a biology class. So I entered the class with the eye of a detective   looked for my mark. There he was, a freshman guy who wanted to become a doctor and I was a cute enough senior who had learned, among other things, the fine art of flirting with an expected gain. So I smiled and asked if he'd like to be my lab partner. Of course he said yes and probably would have even if I'd told him the truth. Which was that I wanted him to do all the bloody yucky cutting and I'll skate thru on your budding skills. And he did and so did I. Then came a really awful experiment that had to do with baby chicks and slits on the necks where we were to insert pellets of some kind. It was no longer enough to have a partner with a wicked scalpel skill, this poor unsuspecting critter was alive! So the day came and just before the experiment began I raised my hand and asked the professor where the line was between justified experimentation and cruelty. He replied,

there isn't one. So I rose from my swivel stool and proclaimed "This is barbarism. You have done this before and are well aware of the results. There is no reason to repeat this act of cruelty to satisfy some class requirement. This is pointless torture. I refuse to take part and will organize a protest outside of Budge Hall that will bring the press and end this act of cruelty once and for all. With that I would storm out of the class as if in fact I had the guts to say any of that in the first place. Instead, I went up to the professor and said I wasn't feeling good and left the freshman future MD to do his butchery. I still wish I could have a redo on that exit.

Myself, my sisters and my brother were blessed with grandparents that lived long enough for us to love them and learn from them. I had a special relationship with my grandfather. He was a well-known respected attorney in the town I grew up in. From the ages of 15 to 24 we exchanged long typed letters with each other. The unusual and unique part of that is that we lived 5 blocks from each other but our best conversations were in written correspondence sent through the United States Post Office. If you are fortunate, there are times in your life when you know someone truly loves you. I knew it when he wrote to me that we were kindred spirits. It was an affirmation in my life that I will always carry with me. He was smart, clever, kind, moral and had a great dry sense of humor. He had this wonderful, gravely voice that made you take a second look at his short, conservatively dressed and unassuming appearance.

I loved him very much.

Through these letters we discussed poetry, politics, family, travel experiences, dreams, worries, human nature and love. At the time I was only slightly aware that he was gently leading and teaching me through this journey that we shared.

At the bottom of each typed letter we would sign our names with a drawing. He good naturedly drew a square to acknowledge his age and that he was not part of the "now" generation. My signature was a bunch of squiggly helter skelter circles and lines to demonstrate my emotional and moral confusion about life and the world around us.

I kept all of the letters. And I reread them from time to time to feel that he is with me still and continuing to teach me how to live a life that will be easier to leave one day because of his guidance and willingness to accept me as a I was.

The group I hung with in high school was a pretty decent bunch of kids. But there is either darkness or just plain stupidity in all of us, especially in high school. One night while riding around in a car full of friends, someone decided we should all go look at the house where the weird guy lived. It was dark and as we approached the house I saw that there were many kids in cars doing the same thing. There was a procession of vehicles slowly passing in front of the house.

There was a light in an upstairs window and the curtains were open. Inside the room you could see a man tracing the outline of the window with his hands. He methodically repeated the outline again and again as if he needed more than anything in the world to touch each peeling inch of it and in the same exact pattern each time. As I stared at him, as did we all, some of the kids stuck their heads out of the car windows and yelled at the man. I don't remember what they said but I know it was cruel and ugly and frightening. As I sat in confused disbelief at what I was unwittingly an accomplice to, I saw his mother come out of the front door. To my horror she started begging us to leave. "My son was in the war and is sick, please go home", she pleaded. The car I was in was sandwiched between others in this degrading carnival atmosphere. I found myself a prisoner unable to leave. I just wanted to disappear as quickly as possible. I wanted to get out of the car and yell at everyone, to somehow stop this ugly parade of darkness and stupidity. But I did nothing. To this day it is an experience that haunts me. We as humans have evolved in so many amazing ways. But not enough and certainly not fast enough.

 Death is an odd thing. When it is time to go a person just leaves. There are often no farewells. It's not like a loved one leaving on a train and waving from the passenger car window. "Bye. I love you! See you soon." There are no reassuring words to let you know that they will be on the other side waiting for you, that they will be happy and safe until you join them. There are no last minute notes to slip into your hand to tell you that even though you can't see them, they will be with you in the shadows and whispers of your day. No, they just slip away from you and in one small breath that is their last, they just aren't anymore, leaving you with your greatest fears and most desperate hopes for something, anything.

No one told me that when I had sufficiently numbed myself in a busy day you would quietly and without warning pass through me and become painfully real and vivid, fleetingly warm and close and that as quickly as you were with me, more completely even then when you were alive, you would be gone.

My daughter Jennie was about 8 years old at the time. Most summer mornings I would take my son and daughter to one of the beaches on Lake Minnetonka. One morning she decided to take her beloved Barbie doll with her. Every new Barbie upon exiting from the box was immediately subjected by Jennie to a chopped hair cut with a pair of scissors. (that's just a visual addition to the story and of no importance). At some point during this Norman Rockwell summer morning at the beach Jennie lost Barbie in the lake. Since Jennie was the only one with any control of the situation, I'm assuming it wasn't Barbie's fault. Jennie, in usual 8-year-old female style, started wailing uncontrollably. My son and I knew well the extent to which this emotional outburst could lead. So, we flew into control mode, rushing to the car to find any loose change between the seats and in the cup holders. We came up with 72 cents and flew back to the scene of the crime. With no hesitation I commanded the attention of all 20 or so kids, moms, dads, grandmas, babysitters and a few households in the adjacent area declaring a 72-cent reward for anyone finding the above mentioned drowning victim with the bad haircut. To my surprise and delight most of them jumped into action forming a human chain running from one beach buoy to the other. It wasn't long before a yelp was emitted from the rescuer who stepped on her out stretch arms. The crowd let out a unified cheer of relief and delivered Barbie to a puffed faced red eyed little girl. I don't remember who received the reward money, but the memory is priceless.

This happened in Mrs Abbott's 10th grade speech class. At least this is the way I remember it happening. I'm sure there are others that were there that day who have their own version of the story and I'm sure one, if not both, of us are wrong to some degree. With that disclaimer I will proceed. It is my personal opinion that all speech classes should be outlawed as cruel and unusual punishment in a high school setting that is already cruel and unusual enough. The class had its mix of cheer leaders, jocks, audio visual guys and kids that had perfected the Darwinian skill of blending into chalk boards in hopes of surviving yet another day in High School Hell. One of the guys in class was Mike (I've changed the name to protect the guilty). He was my first love in grade school but that is another story.

It was the day we were to give our final speech for the big grade at the end of the course and everyone was hoping for an early death or at least the strength to hold down whatever goop we ate in the school lunchroom that day. Each of us was given a general idea as to what our speech should be about. Mrs. Abbott instructed me that my speech was to be humorous. I had a bit of a lip back then and could provoke a laugh here and there in class. But it was one thing to be funny off the cuff and quite another to be told to be funny at a specific time and place. After much thought about dropping out of school and joining the Peace Corp to avoid my comic debut I came up with a plan.

But first it was Mike's turn and I was to follow him and be the last speech given. Mike had just broken up with his current girlfriend and everyone knew all that had happened between them or at least most of the stories we had made up about them. He slowly and very seriously walked up to the front of the class and meticulously laid out several layers of towels on the floor. He then stood on the towels. He started to explain his current breakup with the love of his life who was sitting quietly in the desk next to me. He talked sincerely about his sadness over the loss of something he thought would be a story of love to tell his grand children. But alas that was not to be. And since he could no longer live with the pain of his heartbreak he took out a jackknife and jammed it into his stomach and fell to the floor to commence bleeding. Dead silence covered the room for what seemed an eternity. Finally Mrs Abbott recovered and ran to save Mike and what might be left of her teaching career. No one screamed, as we were in North Dakota and that just isn't seemly. Instead, we watched intensely as she dropped to her knees beside Mike who quickly jumped to his feet, tore open his shirt and revealed the pouch of fake blood he had taped to his stomach. Did I mention he was a drama student? It took a few minutes for everyone to regain their breath and commence pretending the whole thing hadn't happened. Then I was up. Talk about a hard act to follow. But noting the general catatonic expressions on my classmate's faces I was hoping no one was really going to be listening to what I had to say anyway.

So here was my attempt to avoid a humorous speech and please remember the Shakespearian tragedy that had just unfolded in front of the class. *"Thanks for coming folks. I'm sure you all enjoyed the festivities of the evening. Have a safe trip home and before you leave could you please fold up your chairs and line them up against the back wall so the church janitor can mop the floors. You've been a great crowd."* Then I sat down. Needless to say no one laughed. Maybe they would have laughed if Mike hadn't plunged the group into a deep traumatic stupor moments before. And maybe not, but honestly I thought it was pretty clever. I got a C.

So if it is 1964 and you are a 13 year old girl you will do anything to possibly, maybe, get lucky enough to hang with the popular girls. That was me I'm afraid. In the 7th grade you could leave the school building to go home for a half hour lunch. Lunch was rarely on the menu for us. It was more likely that we would grab an ice cream bar from the cafeteria and ditch the building as soon as possible.

One of the popular girls was Jill. She was pretty and rich and a cheerleader. So when she said we had to hurry over to the small family run market by the alley on 8th Avenue during our lunch period to get Beatles cards I was on board. For all I knew they were squished bugs on the Jack of diamond but by golly I faked excitement and hipness and headed over with the group. Of course I hung back once we got there because if you are clueless as to the destination it is best to follow. I may have been clueless but I wasn't totally stupid. As soon as we left the store I sure as heck jumped up and down and screamed like I was on fire, because that's what everyone else did. I was always just a step behind until my senior year in high school when I morphed into 1969 accompanied by The Doors. So the heck with Jill.

With my three sisters I shared the second-floor bedroom of the house we grew up in. It was a story and a half so I should say we shared what looked more like a long skinny tent. One of the two windows overlooked the cement sidewalk leading to the back door. We were told that in case of a fire we should shove a mattress out the small window and jump. That sounded reasonable enough. But being an over thinker from the start I planned on using a belt to secure a pillow to my ass to ensure that the fall would be extra cushy. Good to go.

It was the 60s. We didn't worry about seatbelts. First of all there weren't any and who needed them anyway when Mom could just throw out her arm as she screeched to a stop and save all five of us in one maternal, heroic movement.

We dealt with most dangers with total denial or absolute ignorance. Doctor's visits were reserved for compound fractures and torn arteries. Passed that you just hoped for the best. Frost bit fingers were stuffed into snowbanks. Earaches were treated with Mom blowing smoke from her Raleigh cigarettes into your throbbing ear drum. If you confessed that your arm hurt when you "did this" Mom's remedy was simple "Well, then don't do that!"

Once when one of us was sick we woke Mom up from a dead sleep in the middle of the night to announce that all was not well. Not fully awake, I'm hoping, she replied "Go sit on the dresser". Poor thing, we tormented her with that one for many years to come.

And since no one else admitted to it, nightmares and horrible creatures under the bed were just something that you and only you experienced so just shut up and pray every night that you made it through it. Even the prayer backed you up on the fear that either your dreams or the thing under the bed would get you. If I should die before I wake was more likely to happen than not. We grew up and grew old anyway.

A poem

Why didn't you say goodbye
the January day,
when that damn warring airplane
took you so far away?

Maybe you knew before you left
that you were going to die,
so your heart just wouldn't let you
come and say goodbye.

Please try and understand
I can't come to where you lie,
I guess I feel like you did then
I just can't say goodbye.

Many years have come and gone,
Again it's the month of May.
I went back home to meet your mom
On this Memorial Day

She talked of you as a child and a son,
I told her stories of our youth.
and as we shared our memories and loss
she taught me a simple truth.

She showed me that your memory is alive,
so you'll never really die.
She made me laugh,
She let me cry,
She helped me say goodbye.

I ran away to California in 1969. Really, I took a train and worried the Hell out of my poor parents when I left Grand Forks with my friend Nan. But it was 1969 and I had to go to California. I just had to. We picked Santa Monica as our destination both because it was such a pretty name and because we knew a friend there who would pick us up when we got there and make sure we weren't living on the beach. The first night there was one of a complete suspension of reality. Candy, our California friend, picked us up from the airport in a Ford Mustang and said we were going straight to a beach party. How could this possibly be happening to me? I lived in North Dakota! By the time we arrived at the beach party it was dark and as we sat by the bonfire, I heard the ocean. It was right there but I couldn't see it through the moonless sky. It came over me like a wash of amniotic fluid. I had arrived!

Once we found our bearings, we rented a flea bag house at the end of a horseshoe layout of other flea bag houses. It was sheer heaven, sand fleas and all. We slept with calamine lotion next the mattresses that lay on the floor so that we could coat our legs with it in the middle of the night to dull the itch.

There were four rooms. The kitchen was black with red cupboards and there was a tie die sheet for the living room curtains. The bathroom and tub were mostly black but so much of it was peeling off you could argue the point. This was home. Not necessarily the best neighborhood but three blocks from the beach made it perfect. There were no locks on the windows so we lined up glass drinking glasses on the window sill so that if anyone tried to get in we would at least hear our demise in advance.

The house to our left was rented by a prostitute with a hippie boyfriend. We had an outdoor theater view of her place so when we were bored we would watch as the men came to court her shall we say. Often the hippie boyfriend would exit the back door as the "suitor" entered the front. What fun.

The Brown family lived at the end of the "U" adjoining the sidewalk. They were a Jewish family from the Bronx. Mom was a large woman with a large heart and very few teeth. Dad was a skinny sunbaked guy who spent his days playing chess on the beach with similar sunbaked guys. They had two daughters, Helen and Lillian. The Browns were my education into the life of a rough and tumble Jewish family from the Bronx. The adopted us. I'm guessing they did so because we were two 18 year olds from North Dakota that had victim written all over us. They nick named us Lizzie and Dizzie and made up funny songs about people from North Dakota. I loved them. They were so not the mash potato people I was familiar with all my life. They fed us chicken dinners and this amazing baked macaroni baked pie with sugar crustiness on top.

The neighborhood had a block of retail stores. But not like they are now. These were stores that had been there forever and old people ran them and sat in rocking chairs on the sidewalk just in case someone wanted to buy something. I don't really think they cared one way or the other; it was just nice to sit in the sun and rock. At one of the thrift shops I found a Raggedy Ann and a Raggedy Andy kind of doll that were 35 cents each. We were surviving on 10 cent bananas so it was a real stretch to fork out that kind of cash for something that was a luxury. I bought the girl doll and named her Molly. Forty years later I still have her and wish I could go back in time and buy her best friend. It was a crime to have separated them.

As we looked for jobs we frequented a small corner Jewish deli run by two brothers. We would often get refund money from them for the pop bottles we picked up along the beach. Then we would buy a banana and as much freshly sliced bologna as our pop bottle returns allowed. One day as one of the brothers sliced off meat for me, he paused and asked, "Found a job yet?" I told him I hadn't but was sure I would any day. He glanced up at me and then went back to slicing the meat into a lacey pile that amounted to far more than the pop bottles would cover. I'll never forget his kindness.

And I did get a job shortly afterwards. It was a front desk of a Jewish retirement home called Ocean House. It had previously been a hotel with a pool that they had to cement over because the residents kept falling into it. It was run by a Rabbi and his family and employed mostly Hispanic people and a black maintenance guy named Albert and little old Midwestern me. Between Yiddish and Spanish I rarely knew what anyone was talking about.

Part of my responsibilities was to make announcements over the PA. On my first day of work two four foot nothing ladies sneaked up on me and giggled as one said to the other "I told you she was a gentile". I had never been the exception to the rule before. I had never been the interesting one that didn't fit into the status quo, and it absolutely thrilled me. Finally I was different and not just one more in the sea of Norwegians and Scandinavians I grew up with. It was delightful! And the residents loved me and often showed their affection by giving me quarters and the occasional leftover lunch fruit to fatten me up.

Albert, the maintenance guy, was about 40 years old and didn't talk much to anyone. He probably didn't understand anything anyone was saying either. Nan and I would take excursions into LA so we could send postcards back home to let everyone know that we were worldly and they were not. One afternoon I saw Albert standing on a corner and I got all excited because I actually knew someone in LA! I yelled "Albert" several times and waved my arms to get his attention. There was no way he couldn't hear me. I didn't understand why he ignored me. He finally turned his back and walked the other direction. It took me awhile to figure it out, but I think he knew it wasn't such a good idea to be talking to an 18 year old white girl. I would like to think I'm wrong but I don't think so. Anyway, I never put him in that spot again and we just continued the status quo of not talking to each other.

Oh and then there was Charles Manson. At the time we were living there one of the trials of the century was going on. We managed to find our way to the court house but after pushing every elevator button just to see what each floor looked like we decide we were fish out of water and left. I regret that and so did my lawyer grandfather when he heard we high tailed it out of there. No guts no glory.

Cars. After you've lived enough decades they become markers in your life. They are a way of categorizing events, locations and memories. The first car I remember was a brown Nash Lafayette circa 1940s. It was old and brown and round and I loved it. Most exciting events happened because of this garage dwelling family member. When I was little the slow expansion of the world happened when my sisters and I were tossed into the backseat with anticipation of great events to come. Mostly the destination was the grocery store or the gas station but at that age it didn't take much to ignite the travel lust I would later discover to be one of my most unfulfilled goal. Around the age of seven I found out my parents were selling it. I was shocked and bewildered. After all, it was the only car I had ever known and I thought once you had a car it was yours forever. How could they sell this wheeled extension of our lives? It shook the very core of my sense of security. What was next: the house, my sisters, me? I sneaked into the garage just before dark, kissed it ever so gently on the hood and sadly bid it farewell.

Grandma had a 1948 black Dodge with suicide doors. I was in grade school at the time, but I somehow knew that it was a pretty cool car, or at least could have been. It had beautiful brown knobs on the radio and all that other stuff I didn't understand on the dashboard. Grandma was a hard working depression era woman so when you climbed into the back seat to go to the Dairy Queen you had to move junk around and rest your feet on paint cans. This was a workhorse of a car. I heard stories of Grandma driving under the underpass on Washington Street and losing a mattress tied to the top ensnarling what in the 60s qualified as a traffic jam in Grand Forks. She also used it to pull a lawn mower from one location to another while it was tied to the back bumper. Later my cousin Doug acquired it, gutted It, and drove it around town using a kitchen chair as the driver's seat. It was the 60's; you could get away with that kind of stuff.

When my grandparents bought a new car my dad bought their old black Buick Roadmaster from them. Large and sleek with a look of the mafia, it was christened "the Black Beast" by my friend who would never return from Vietnam. The most important detail of the car was this amazing armrest that you could pull out of the middle of the back seat. This was true luxury. But in our family of five kids it practically doubled as a child seat so that the vertically underdeveloped could take in the scenery.

Back to the mafia connection, as the Buick aged it started to resemble Don Corleone just before he died in the movie "The Godfather". Bruised and battered but still moving, it started to announce its arrival a good block or two before it came into sight. My rather large father wore in the driver's seat to the point that if his petite teenage daughters were to drive the car, they needed to sit on a couple of old couches cushions to see between the horn and the steering wheel. To add to the creative motoring, the seat spring had sprung so that the only position was all the way back. So now you had to add a few bed pillows behind your back, or for shorter distances you would hang on the steering wheel with all your strength and hope you didn't lose your grip going around the corners.

Enter the 1956 yellow and white Ford Fairlane that always reminded me of a large lemon on wheels. We bought it for $210.00 from a couple that won a new car in a contest. Years later we sold it to a hippy that painted it up with flowers and tie die patterns and drove it all over the country and into the ground. It is the only car I really wish I'd kept.

Then came the 1964 Nash Rambler. Most of us have memories of our first romantic experience in a car. And this vehicle held mine. It was a tank of a car. One day I was sitting on Gateway Drive with my mom, waiting to make a left turn to the A&W Drive Inn to pick up my sister after work when I was rear-ended by a Corvette. The accident put a permanent crick in my neck, a small dent in the trunk of the Rambler and totaled the Corvette. Well, not quite. In a shocked daze I stared into my rear view mirror, watched the driver get out and angrily break off the only undamaged piece left on the car, the antenna. Who in their right mind would buy a plastic car! The answer: the uninsured guy who hit me and then tried to date me.

And then there was the red 1957 Studebaker station wagon. It won no prize for gas mileage getting eight miles to the gallon if you were lucky. Good thing we lived in a small town. One winter I got hit by another car at the intersection of Cottonwood and 10th which was half a block from home. The accident shattered not only my driver's side window but also my belief that I would live forever. When asked by the police officer if I was sure I wasn't speeding I reassured him I couldn't have been going more than 10 miles an hour because it took up to four blocks to maximize at a breakneck speed of 25 mph. When it snowed I would have to shovel out the car before I could get in and sit on a frozen seat with no hope of heat in the car because the window was now in a permanent state of openness. Years later when I told someone this story, they asked "why didn't you put plastic over the window?" Good question, for which I had no answer that would possibly clear me of being stupid.

The white Chevy Corvair was an experience. Looked cool but that was it. It was a manual which was challenging enough without having one of the gears in the up position randomly falling out of place. It would just fall down. When I would turn a corner, which happens, I would turn the wheel using only my left hand because my right hand was busy holding the stick shift in the up position. We learned to love a challenge.

And what great memories were had of a 1963 Ford Falcon. My best friend and I bought it for $140.00 in Santa Monica California in the summer of love, 1969. Really it was 1970, but 1969 sounds cooler and does a better job of getting the point across. Nan and I tried our hand at fleeing the Midwest and spreading our liberated hippie wings in a flea infested clay roofed 1920's four room house two blocks off the beach. After the experience became more work than we expected we bought the Falcon to return to the rest of our lives. Nan was the artist half of the relationship and before departing on our grand road trip she painted the back windshield with little footprints and "keep on truckin" to complete our gypsy statement. Many years later we may not have the Falcon, but we still have each other and a black and gold California license plate.

The Opal Cadett. Yes, there was such a car; I'm not making it up. Mom loved that car so much that when it died she wanted to have it crushed up and put in the living room as a coffee table. Another car (I'm not making this up) was my sister's graduation present from Grandpa and Grandma. It was a Simca. It was a cute little car but just a hiccup in the history of automobiles.

Now I drive new cars that are well maintained and brought in for repairs immediately when the slightest problem arises. They are safe, efficient, reliable and boring.

 My first concert was in 1966 when my friend Becky's mother took us to Fargo to see the Beach Boys. I remember them singing "In My Room" and they spoke to me and only me about what it was like to be 16 in 1966. I don't remember any of the other songs. But what I do remember is standing in the crowded entrance of the building and waiting to go in. There was a young man in the crowd that had a long ponytail tied neatly behind his head. The crowd started to heckle him with rude comments like "need a pair of scissors?" "Hey girlie", and "Let's take him to a barber". Remember this was North Dakota in 1966 and the world was just a step ahead of us. The guy stood there silently and said nothing back. After who know s how long of this abuse he turned and left the lobby. I wondered if he took the next train to California. I hoped so. He is mostly what I remembered about the concert.

In 1968 my grandparents drove me to Chicago to stay with cousins for a week. We ended up going to a concert in a pavilion on Lake Delavan to see Archie Bell and the Drells. There were black lights and no one told me that the lights highlighted the lotion you smeared on your face making you look like an abstract painting. Or that even if you went to the bathroom to wash it off you still looked pretty silly. But the best part was this Jewish guy that I ended up sitting with outside the pavilion on the grass under that warm summer night. He talked to me about how the world could be changed in an instant if we collectively decided to be kind to each other. He was amazing. I was hooked. I was mesmerized. I was seventeen. On the way home I told my grandparents about the experience with the same enthusiasm of the Jewish boy. My grandfather let out a laugh and immediately saw the embarrassed and slightly disappointed look on my face. He quickly looked me in the eyes and said "I am not laughing at you. I would never do that. My laugh is one of joy that such idealism still exists in this world and most importantly In you." I don't remember much of the concert.

Three years later my best friend and I left the plains and went to California. We went to a Rod McKuen concert at the Hollywood Bowl. We took a bus from Santa Monica and failed to get off at the right bus stop. The bus driver pulled over on the shoulder of a busy freeway and let us off to take our chances with the traffic by crossing over the four lanes of traffic and walking over the landscaped edges to the theater. We must have looked like ducks in a shooting gallery. I caught the look on his face and it was one of deep concern; either concern for our lives or concern for the trouble he'd be in for letting us off on the side of the freeway.

As we waited for the concert to begin we marveled at the fact that we were actually sitting at the Hollywood Bowl. We watched the roadies work and I wondered about how exciting it must be to be on the stage setting up all the equipment for famous stars. But they didn't look too excited and it occurred to me that it might just be a job. After the concert someone offered us a ride home in the back of a pickup. We laid in the back of the truck bed and looked up at the California sky which is so much more beautiful than the North Dakota sky when you are eighteen. I don't remember much of the concert.

Then there was "Hair". Let's just say I wasn't that experienced and when a naked man stepped over my theater chair I lost some of my midwestern innocence.

It was around 1970. My best friend and I attended a free Arlo Guthrie concert at the Santa Monica Civic Center. "Free" being the only reason we were there in this huge auditorium with only about 20 other financially strapped clones. Arlo came out with his guitar and a folding chair. He politely thanked the rag tag group for attending. But before he sang, he introduced a speaker that would open for him. A young, thin man in an ill-fitting black suit came out to plead his case and request contributions to help fund the Irish Republican Army. He received a wealth of blank stares from the attendees that most likely had just had lunch off the proceeds from the pop bottles we'd gathered from the beach and returned for money. Poor guy he was definitely asking the wrong crowd. Then Arlo gave in and started singing. One of us hollered out "play Alice's Restaurant!" He said he was sick of the song and if we wanted to hear it we would have to sing it to him. He picked up the mike, brought it to the edge of the stage, aimed it towards us and sat back down to listen to us sing the first bit of the song until the last person ran out of the lyrics that were remembered. That motley rendition of the song was followed by an audience member throwing a lit joint up onto the stage. Well, what can I say, it was the age of Aquarius. He glanced cautiously around the back of the auditorium and then partook in the only donation of the night. Definitely one of the most memorable of concerts for sure.

Fast forward to 1979 at a Moody Blues concert when I was five months pregnant with my daughter and for the first time I felt her move. It was magical. I told my mom about it and she replied, "The music was too loud, the baby was probably trying to get the heck out of there." Guess what, I don't remember much the concert.

One more and I promise I'm done. In 1994 my daughter experienced her first death as she watched her friend get hit by a car and die. That week my husband and I went to a concert. We already had the tickets and I think we felt we needed the short distraction. I could think of nothing else but my daughter's fresh pain, her loss of innocence and a future that would forever be scarred by this tragic experience. I cried through much of the concert. That is what I remember.

So, I figured out that I am genetically hard wired to see the world through the human experience. People are what fascinate me; us, in all our glory and wonder and awfulness. It doesn't mean we shouldn't go to concerts. They are a fun exclamation point in the sameness of our days. But don't forget to look around you and observe and hopefully learn from what we are all going though alone, together.

Made in the USA
Monee, IL
25 January 2025

10959275R00100